Not All Angels Fly...

JOSEPH ANNAMKUTTY JOSE

Not All Angels Fly...

You Could Be One!

Translated from the Malayalam by

Hrishikesh Mundani

DC Books

HARPER NON-FICTION

Published by DC Books in Malayalam 2019
This English edition published in India by Harper Non-Fiction 2025
An imprint of HarperCollins *Publishers*
HarperCollins *Publishers* India, Cyber City,
Building 10-A, Gurugram, Haryana – 122002, India
www.harpercollins.co.in
By arrangement with DC Books

2 4 6 8 10 9 7 5 3 1

P-ISBN: 978-93-6989-288-4
E-ISBN: 978-93-6989-038-5

Typeset in 11/14.7 Adobe Caslon Pro
by HarperCollins *Publishers* India Pvt. Ltd

Printed and bound at
Thomson Press (India) Ltd

MIX
Paper | Supporting responsible forestry
FSC® C010615

This book is produced from independently certified FSC® paper to ensure responsible forest management.

HarperCollins *Publishers*, Macken House, 39/40 Mayor Street Upper, Dublin 1, D01 C9W8, Ireland

To Lionel Messi,

Waiting for your late-night Champions League matches gave me the perfect quiet hours to write this book

CONTENTS

TRANSLATOR'S NOTE

Daivathinte Charanmar's immense, record-breaking success in Malayalam could only be the second-most significant reason for its translation. I recall realizing this while translating the semi-autobiographical accounts in this book. The primary reason, I would argue, is that at the heart of nearly every chapter lies an essence, an emotion, an awareness, an inclusive sensitivity, a latent element of transcendence even, that permeates through all language barriers and geographical boundaries—something universal.

The simplicity of the narrative is nearly deceptive. It leads readers to believe these are not ideas they haven't already known, seen, or heard. Yet, by the time they finish reading, they may catch themselves contemplating, 'I had known this, but did I truly understand it? I had heard it all before, but how much did I really comprehend? I had seen it, but did I pay enough attention?' The book's exploration of human themes is sure to connect with every reader, making them feel understood, as if it were written specifically for them.

'Going with the Flaw' was the working title of this book, and it was no accident. The book boldly exposes flaws of all kinds: personal, rational, relational, social, generational, intellectual, emotional and existential. What's intriguing is that it doesn't even spare the author himself! In stories where he is the focal point, he doesn't hesitate to dissect his own life and mistakes, laying them bare for the reader to see. As Joseph reveals himself in many places, readers may find their own reflections, stemming from the collective thread that weaves through the chronicles, prompting a strange introspection that is challenging, yet rewarding.

The chapter 'My Double Shame' invokes a contemplation on one's mother and is sure to move, even if fleetingly, the most unsentimental reader. 'Feminichi' explores societal attitudes towards feminism; its unnerving sketches hit prevalent perspectives painfully close to the bone. 'Watchman of Life' begins as the story of an ordinary man but gradually unravels the complex interplay of the debatable political ideologies and subtleties that shape the scrupulousness of this land, shedding light on the often overlooked acts of heroism by everyday people. 'Love that Goes Unloved' delves into the unfairness of unrequited love, exploring specific aspects of sibling rivalry and evolving family dynamics. Chapters like 'The Demolition Man' and 'Missed by a Hair' provide much-needed light-heartedness, offering readers well-deserved laughter. 'The Cool Confession' feels like a fresh breeze and inventively redefines repentance. 'Saintly Soft Porn' looks at the most primal struggle of humanity straight in the eye, making one wonder about the demarcation between sin and sainthood. 'Friendship, Love, Life' meanders through existential crisis and the complex definition of true love.

Not All Angels Fly makes one ponder: are human flaws the only absolute truth? Is perfection merely a carefully crafted, well-intentioned lie that the majority has agreed upon? Perhaps not all the time, but often? This is one of the significant questions that the book continually raises. The stories encourage you to examine whether humans genuinely have as much freedom of choice as they like to believe. Are we capable of being flawless, or is it wiser to navigate our imperfections? Is striving for perceived perfection while acknowledging our flaws a more sensible approach? Should we set out to battle each flaw within us, or should we learn to manage them better, thus 'going with the flaw'?

Joseph Annamkutty Jose's writing style is almost inimitable, to say the least. What makes it so? As one reads through the chapters, it becomes increasingly clear that instead of 'writing stories', he strives to 'tell stories' to the reader—it is as if he is always speaking to them. This is not surprising, given that he is one of the most sought-after public speakers of his language. When the characters converse, you can hear the writer's voice in the background. The writer also speaks directly to the reader, sharing his viewpoints, stating his opinions, and even offering suggestions on what to do and what not to do! This has often left me puzzled because every translator is a reader first. As a reader, I must admit that, at places, I paused to ask myself, 'Isn't this a bit patronizing? Preachy?' But I landed on a different conclusion after I combed through the entire book and stayed afloat on its currents. I realized that his style leans more towards speaking than traditional writing. Writing can often be a very calculated process; you write, rewrite, proofread, edit, re-edit, improve, improvise, and do many things before finalizing the lines that readers get to read. But how does it work when a speaker on stage addresses a live crowd? It goes straight from his mind to his mouth, then to the ears of the audience. There is not much scope for tactical tailoring. It could be this naked honesty that makes Joseph's voice stand out.

In this era of political correctness and verbal ironing, an author writing his heart out is a rare instance. When a writer finds the courage to be himself and let his stained characters be themselves, his words shine through in their rarity. The joy and the challenge of translating his stories lay in this factor. He uses analogies that may not seem like typical choices for writers. Throughout the book, he references popular Malayalam movies and sprinkles the text with dialogues from them, which perfectly fit the situations in the stories.

To get these regional nuances across to non-Malayali readers, or even Malayali readers who aren't avid followers of mainstream Malayalam cinema, made translating these stories a challenge. But having said that, this conversational style is one of the critical elements that gives his words their unorthodox freshness. In the end, the mass appeal of his writing lies in the fact that even if we do away with the local references, or replace them with more globally understandable substitutes in English, the spirit of the stories remains unruffled!

Although it wasn't entirely intentional, in retrospect, it looks like I have always considered the reader my top priority. I find myself asking, why is that? The translator's central commitment is to the book, the characters and the world its chapters contain, and, of course, to the author's original work, which the translator is tasked with doing justice to. But when everything is said and done, aren't journeys primarily about the travellers themselves? More than the tour planners, the guides, the baggage handlers, the drivers, the street vendors, the routes, the route maps, the compasses, or the destinations themselves, isn't every tour mostly about the tourist? Isn't it about what the travellers experience with their emotional, intellectual and sensory faculties, more than whatever they are provided with by anyone at any point during the journey?

Daivathinte Chaaranmaar, by Joseph Annamkutty Jose, did not come out of a conventional literary framework; it is rather an assemblage of human journeys, short and long. Yes, every chapter is a trip that the reader takes—a voyage from one sensation to another, an old opinion to a new one, a blurred view to a crystal-clear image, a tinge of tension to a whiff of peace, to some integral people, towards integrity, to the good, to the evil and back, to godforsaken situations, to the good God, to hope, to redemption, and on and on. As the translator of this much-loved book written originally in Malayalam, I have made an earnest effort to recreate the sensations of those journeys, tangible or possibly otherwise. Rather than trying to pinch, pick and place every inch or replicate every yard, the attempt has been to ensure that the long miles of it were as enjoyable as the original, and that even the remotely placed milestones were not missed.

When we say Joseph took the reader on a separate journey with every chapter, one may wonder, what was the vehicle? His vehicle was the language he wrote in, Malayalam. With this book, we will embark on the same journey but on a different vehicle: English. The comforts and cushioning of this one may differ from the original; its windowpanes may have slightly different tints, its seats may recline a little less or a little more, its air conditioning temperatures may vary and its engine may sound different when it rumbles. But we will try to make up for all that by adjusting how we handle the steering wheel of this language, shifting its gears sensibly, accelerating smoothly and braking softly, and promptly parking at the sunrise and sunset points Joseph has prepared for us. Let's take a drive through the landscapes Joseph shaped, observing the structures he erected and the roads he paved, greeting the people he placed along the sidewalks, resting under the intermittent shade trees he planted, and enjoying the winds of life he set in motion through his one-of-a-kind book.

So, it's time to board and move forward as we wind down, meeting some exemplary souls and hearing their stories. Each bears their blemishes, yet they remind us that whatever burdens them does not diminish their essence; they stand out in their uniqueness. Still, the question remains whether they are 'angels' from any perspective. They don't appear ethereal or possess enchanting halos or captivating wings. They certainly aren't airborne! It's fair to think that even if they are angels of some unusual category, they are all flawed! But remember our discussion on going with the flaw? Who knows, when we walk alongside them for a while, we may realize that despite being flawed, they might still be angels of no lesser order. And who knows, at some unexpected juncture, we might agree with the title of this book and say, 'Yes, not all angels fly.'

PREFACE

The concept of angels has always fascinated me. My earliest memory of an angel comes from a Christmas crib—an ethereal figure with wings, hovering protectively over baby Jesus. As a child, I believed angels were guardians of goodness, beings who shielded us from harm. I often wished for one to guide and protect me.

But life, as I've come to realize in my thirties, is more nuanced. Sometimes, an angel doesn't wear wings or bring immediate joy. Occasionally, they arrive as challenges, frustrations, or even pain. It's all about perspective—what if we could shift the way we see angels?

Let me share an example. In 2012, during my first job in China, I experienced my loneliest Christmas. My boss had promised I could go home to India but, at the last moment, asked me to stay back due to an emergency. Stranded in a foreign land, far from family and friends, I despised him for it. Social media wasn't as vibrant back then, so I coped by pouring my feelings into a blog I titled *Buried Thoughts*. Little did I know, this blog would become the foundation of my first book, a bestseller of the same name. And who helped me publish it? That very boss I once loathed. Life has a curious way of revealing its hidden angels, doesn't it?

This experience taught me that angels might not always appear as benevolent figures. They could be people, situations or incidents that, while seemingly harsh or insignificant at first, later transform our lives in profound ways.

Each of us has played the role of an angel, knowingly or unknowingly. Perhaps you recommended a friend for a job that became their big break. Or maybe you made a split-second decision while driving that saved a life. Angels aren't mythical beings—they're moments, choices and acts of kindness that ripple through lives.

We can't create angels, but we can become them. Often, we don't notice them when looking ahead, but a glance backward reveals their presence. This book is my retrospective journey, a collection of twenty-one stories about the angels in my life—ordinary people and events that shaped me in extraordinary ways. These angels didn't have fairy-tale wings, but they carried hearts full of grace.

Why should you read this book? Perhaps it will inspire you to revisit your own story and discover the angels you never knew existed. Maybe it will challenge your perspective on life, happiness and gratitude. After all, the true meaning of life often lies in appreciating the path we've walked, rather than obsessing over the road ahead.

Not All Angels Fly is my humble attempt to share these discoveries with you. As I introduce my angels, I hope you'll find your own. And even if you don't, perhaps this book will inspire you to become someone else's angel.

Are you ready for a high-five from angels?

THE COOL CONFESSION

'We don't sign superstars, we make them.'

—ARSENE WENGER

It happens to some of us all the time. We can recall the faces of many people whose lives improved because they listened to our words. People who strapped themselves to some advice we handed out and got airlifted from the dark dungeons of life. But, on the other hand, we remained in the same place where we happily waved them off to safer meadows. It is not just me; I have also encountered other people whose destinies seem all about being Balettan—in the Malayalam movie by the same name, the great actor Mohanlal plays the protagonist, Balettan, who is quick to help anyone he possibly can but fails to handle his own life fittingly.

The movie, *Gandhi, My Father*, came out in 2007. It was based on the life of Harilal Gandhi, Mahatma Gandhi's son. The movie's poster carried a powerful hook that grabbed attention: 'One family's tragedy was the price of a nation's freedom.' Gandhi suffered incontestable personal losses when he made his country's independence the sole purpose of his life. The gashes on his family ran bone deep. Revelry around the birth of the world's largest democracy drowned out the whimpers of a family whose hopes for normalcy had been crushed under a nation's crusade for freedom. While turning his life into a catapult that could hurl India to liberation, Gandhi overstretched his personal world, causing irreversible damage. An article I had read in *Outlook* about Harilal Gandhi comes to mind: It was titled 'The Prodigal Who Didn't Return'.

Guilt snowballed within me.

I decided to confess before it became hefty enough to bury me too deep into inaction. My mind warned me like my old kindergarten teacher: 'Enough, Joseph, now be a good boy!' I went to the Dharmaaram Monastery near Christ College. The receptionist had an air of seriousness about him. 'Are any Fathers available?' I asked. 'I would like to confess.'

He looked at the sun glowering outside the window. 'Chap, does anyone come to confess at noon? Aren't there more appropriate timings for such things?' Disdain underlined every word in his question.

'Brother, it has been really long since I felt such an urge to revive myself. This is a seminary, so there must be some Father, right? It's okay even if it is an elderly Father. Could you please check?' I asked with utmost humility.

'When a sinner repents, heaven rejoices, right? You go wait in the church. This is the time when Fathers would usually be napping, but let me still check. And listen, you may leave if I don't come back within fifteen minutes.' His tone dampened my optimism, but the way he garnished his reply with a biblical verse helped. He showed me the way to the church.

'Oh God, who never forsakes one who prays.' I entered the church, repeating the good old prayer. The coolness of the marble under my feet felt like an old memory. 'Long time no see, Joseph,' the floor accused me.

I sat on a wooden bench. Flipping through a few Mass books lying around, I came across one with the name 'Bro. Palakkudi' on it. Nostalgia nudged me in the ribs. I was a seminary guy once. We seminarians were addressed by our family names back then. I used to have a book with my name written on it: 'Bro. Koottungal'. When I left the seminary, I also left that book and my Bible behind. Are those still intact somewhere in the seminary? If so, with whom? I was absorbed in these thoughts when I heard approaching footsteps.

'You came to confess, right?' A young Father stood smiling at me, wearing a white robe with a cloth tied around his waist.

'Yes.'

'Have you prepared for the confession? Shall we get rolling if you are prepped up and cool to go?'

Priests seldom spoke like that. I have never been asked by one if 'we could get the confession rolling'. I took to his words instantly; they had such style and ease to them.

'Father, you ask me if I am prepared, but I don't really know. I yearned to address and admit to a few things; it felt like I couldn't move an inch ahead unless I confessed. That is when I came running.' I was fidgety.

'The desire to confess is in itself the best preparation for a good confession. Are you particular that you want to confess inside the confessional?'

'Father, confessions are usually done in confessionals, right?' I tried to sound matter-of-fact.

'I mean, if being on your knees is not difficult for you, we shall go to the confessional. Otherwise, you can confess sitting right here. The point is that you should be relaxed and comfortable.' Once again, the Father sounded in alignment with the coolness he seemed to radiate.

'This is indeed one Gen Next Father,' I remember thinking.

'In that case, we shall sit here,' I said with a smile.

'May the almighty God bless you to confess your sins.'

After drawing a cross in the air, he sat there with his head tilted, eyes closed and ears sharp.

I began. 'Father, I have no idea if what I am about to say is a sin, but I feel guilty about some things that I have been doing and I wish to correct all of that.'

'Go ahead, dude. Just tell me what is troubling you.' The Father didn't seem to be a fan of intricate intros.

I stopped beating around the bush and got going.

'Father, I cleared my Plus Two exams, scoring 92 per cent. There are many good colleges back at my place. Regardless of that, if I was sent here for such an expensive education, the sole reason was Chettan's compulsion. Once I joined my college here, Chettan always ensured that I was never short of anything. Still, I lazed around and scored a skimpy 55 per cent in the first semester.

'My family and folks were up in arms. Some scolded me, the rest advised me to resist temptations and defy distractions. Even the response from my brother's friends was not any different: "Right when you sent him off to Bangalore, we were sure the chap would cut loose." But all that Chettan said was, "It's okay; you just try harder next time."'

'And? Did you score well next time?'

'Father, that next time is next week. My second semester exams are about to commence. I haven't started studying yet. And, this time, it won't stop at low marks. I don't think I'll pass the exams. Please help me.'

'You are done? Is that all?'

'Father, like I said, I came running owing to sheer guilt. I don't know if what I confessed is a sin, but there is one more thing: I spent most of the money that Chettan gave me on junk food and soft drinks. Cans after cans of Coke. Pizza after pizza. I knew the money came from his hard-earned salary, still I blew the rest of it on costly movie tickets and huge popcorn buckets. How do I put it? I was being heartlessly extravagant. Been a "prodigal brother", if it is correct to say so. All that being done, I am feeling extremely miserable now, Father.'

Father looked up once; he let out a short hum of acknowledgement. Then he looked straight at me.

'What is your name?'

'Joseph.'

'Josappe, what you confessed is not a sin or anything. But it is something which has even more gravity than a sin. Indolence. You have extreme languor. You have the desire to change, to study, and all that. But you are just out-and-out lazy. Right?'

I didn't expect someone to skin my fat emotional beast of a confession so easily. The Father placed its skeleton, washed and cleaned, on the table for me to see. He was right. When the meat of sloppiness and sentimentality was flayed away, sheer lassitude lay at the core of my wrongdoing. The directness of the Father's interpretation caught me unawares.

'Yes, sort of. I mean, kind of … Ya … somewhat largely so …' I trailed off lamely. But I was there to face the facts. Remorse was running high, driving me insane, and only a shot of truth could act as an antidote.

'Josappe, even I am a student. Doing an MA in English here at Christ College. I have a paper to present in the coming week. You know what? I haven't written a single line of that yet. If this paper is not approved, I will be in a real soup! What I am trying to say is, both of us are sort of in the same boat. So, whatever I am about to tell you is for my own ears as well. What if it helps me too? There is only one way in front of both of us.'

'What is it?'

'Dude, there is this tale in the Bible, right? The vineyard and the farmers. Remember how the story went? In the morning, a bunch of people come to the vineyard for work. The farmer agrees to the wage they demand and lets them in for work. Another group comes sometime later and he hires them as well, agreeing on the payment they want. In the last working hour of that day, a couple of workers come. And what does the farmer do? He hires them, too! And wages? As much as they asked for. At the end of the day, the man who came first and the man who came last were given equal wages. The ones who came first whined, "We came in the morning, worked through the day, toiled in the scorching sun. But you considered the effort of the worker who came in the last hour to be as good as ours?" Now, tell me, Joseph. What did the farmer reply to that complaint?'

'"Didn't I pay you what you asked for? How much I pay the person who came last is my choice. Why do you make a fuss about that."' I paused and looked at the Father to be sure, then continued, 'Wasn't it something on those lines?'

'Spot on! So, dude, how about applying the same story to our situations now? We are the workers who came in last. We have one week ahead of us to really "work". Like that last hour before the sun sets in the vineyard! Why don't we both try studying hard for once? God is a big-hearted farmer. We may get the wage we ask for; who can say we won't? Dude, after all, isn't He the man who fed five thousand people with just five pieces of bread He had? In the one week we have, we will study steadfastly, putting blood and soul into it. That effort should be like our offering to Him. An effort more intense than a prayer! What if the miracle of five thousand happens in our lives too!'

Listening to him was like being plunged underwater. Clarity emerged from the silence that surrounded us and it took me a few moments before I could speak.

'Father, your words seem to have made an instant impact! Suddenly, I am feeling kind of confident. I must say, the hopelessness has vanished altogether.'

'In that case, both of us should make a couple of decisions right now. The first decision is not to waste a moment more feeling sad over the lost time; stick to that strictly. The second: This week, we study, as much as we possibly can, as we've done never before!'

The Father had lit up my spirit with hope.

'And instead of drinking Coke, drink carrot juice. Excellent for one's eyes. You won't feel guilty about wasting money, either. Not just that, aren't you grown up enough to know that these drinks are crazy unhealthy?'

'Yes, Father. I will keep that in mind. But you did not yet tell me what I should do as penance?'

'Study hard for a week. Drink fruit juice instead of Coke.'

I couldn't help but laugh. It was the first time that I laughed during a confession. It was also the first time I was prescribed an atonement that was so practical. But then, with this Father, I should have known.

'Just pray for me too,' the Father blessed me.

While leaving the church, I could feel the extremely studious student within me awakening from the deep slumber that had trapped me since I moved here. I felt unshackled, to say the least. I could feel my insides rumble, ready to go. Glued to the chair, I worked my guts out for a week. The exams went better than usual. The results came out in the middle of the third semester and I had secured 480 marks. That put me in the distinction category with a percentile of 80.

Eager and excited, I called Chettan first. 'I told you that you would rock! We will have a blast tonight,' he replied. Pride and joy blended together in his tone.

We celebrated that night. Back home, Appan and Amma were extremely happy. They celebrated the return of their prodigal son. It was almost after a week that I remembered the Father of Dharmaaram monastery. I felt it was basic courtesy to go meet him and tell him about my exams. At the monastery's reception, the same old, grave-looking receptionist stood. Oddly enough, I didn't know the Father's name yet, and I didn't know who precisely to ask for.

'Brother, you remember me coming here a few months ago, when the sun was scorching and all the Fathers were sleeping? I mean to say, at noon. I wanted to confess and you quoted a biblical verse before going to find a Father to hear my confession? Remember? What was the name of that Father?'

The man gave me a very confused look. I should have constructed my query better, I realized. I looked at him and could sense how blank he was. His stare seemed to command me to simplify and repeat whatever I had just said.

'Brother, there is a young Father here, right? A Father studying English at Christ College. I forgot his name.'

'Chap, there are many young Fathers here, every single one of them studying something somewhere. How to find a person if you ask an ambiguous question like this? Go find his name by some means and come back.'

I was a little disappointed. Walking out of the reception, I felt like visiting the church in Dharmaaram, where I had prayed the last time.

When I stepped on the church floor, I experienced something like an oxymoron: It had a warm coolness or a cool warmness. I experienced a unique joy—the kind that arises when we return to places where we once shed tears, now smiling brightly. I stood there and relished that feeling for some time. I thanked God. Then, while making my way back to my college, I saw a bunch of youngsters playing in the nearby basketball court. Among them, I spotted him, the young Father I had confessed to!

I recall feeling a lot happier than I can probably explain now. I ran towards the court, where he was playing with the college students.

'Excuse me, Father,' I called out aloud. At first, he didn't recognize me.

'Father, I am Joseph. Three months ago, I had come to confess. Do you remember by any chance?'

'Josappe. Ya, I do remember you. How did things turn out?'

'The results are out and I secured 80 per cent. I came to meet you and thank you.'

As he was speaking to me, the students playing with him frequently called out, 'Come on, Father, stay in the game!'

'Give me a minute,' he replied, gesturing with a raised hand.

'Josappe, keep going. Anyway, I am happy that you came all this way to let me know. Alright then, let me get back to the game,' he said to me while beginning to jog back to the court.

'Okay then, Father. You please continue. Have a good day, Father.'

I started to leave when I remembered.

I turned around and asked loudly, 'Father, what about that paper of yours?'

'Pass it, dude, put a three-pointer, shoot!' Passing the ball to the next player, the Father came running to me, panting.

'Josappe, that paper bombed colossally; I will have to repeat it. Could not take it anywhere in a week, but next time, it should be a cakewalk, just plain sailing!' He winked and gave me a thumbs up before going back and resuming the game.

I stayed there staring at that young Father for a while. Some people are like that. They only know how to make others win; they see victory in their own lives rarely. In the movie *Pranchiyettan & the Saint*, Pranchi decides to sponsor Paulie, a student who is uninterested in studies and likely to fail in Class Ten. After committing to take responsibility for Paulie's tuition costs, Pranchi holds the boy close and says something profound.

'Paulie, my boy, the tenth standard and the examination that we are talking about ... even I have not passed that. But if someone else wins in a place where I had lost, and if I can be the reason behind them winning, then that victory is mine as well!'

Dearest Father, I have no idea why I missed out on asking your name even the second time we met. Today, I have the story of our confession written here like this. Would you have read this already? Among a thousand confessions you would have heard by now, would you have remembered mine? I have only one thing to say: My life at present bears an uncanny resemblance to our confession that day. A lot of people are getting reformed through my writing and videos. But I swear (upon my mother, just in case you are not sure if I mean this!), the things I tell people aren't helping *me* much! Once I return to my house, when it is just me inside those walls of my room, I am still burdened by guilts of several kinds. Confessionals are what I am still looking for incessantly, all along my way. But I am trying hard to be a better guy tomorrow. In a place where we don't win, if we are the reason why someone else wins, that victory is ours as well!

Right, Father?

MY DOUBLE SHAME

'Some feelings sink so deep into the heart that only loneliness can help you find them again. Some truths are so painful that only shame can help you live with them.'

—GREGORY DAVID ROBERTS, *SHANTARAM*

I heard this anecdote from Father Bobby. A little girl won first place in a music competition. Curious, Father Bobby asked her parents, 'From which one of you did your daughter inherit her singing?'

The girl's dad replied, 'Neither of us sing, Father. My dad was a labourer in the quicklime plant. Every day after work, he would have a few swigs of arrack and come back home, singing at the top of his throat, oblivious to the world around him. My mother and I used to rebuke him, "Can you please stop this goddamn drunk singing of yours?" Perennially dismissive of the beauty of his singing, we stomped over his source of harmless joy. Dad died a few years ago. Now, when I see my little daughter singing so well, I can't help but think that it is my dad singing out all the songs he couldn't ever sing freely.' The man's voice cracked with guilt and regret. Most of us are haunted by the echoes of abrasive words we have hurled at the people we love in acts of mundane cruelty. Time, distance and destiny separate us from those burnt by our words, crushing even the last hope of redemption. Late realizations, and delayed repentance, change perspectives.

Gandhi's autobiography has a chapter titled 'My Double Shame'. The initial disdain the chapter evoked in me for the Mahatma later transmuted into reverence. Gandhi's father's health is rapidly on the decline and the family knows that he might not make it through the night. Gandhi is tending to his father, massaging the old man's feet. Yet, his mind cannot help but be drawn towards his young wife, Kasturba, asleep just a wall away. As the night draws on, the Mahatma yields to the lure of youth and goes to Kasturba, leaving his father's bedside. Sometime later, a knock on the door breaks the young couple's embrace. 'Father has passed away,' someone cries out on the other side of the door. Gandhi's heart writhes with shame and grief. Despite becoming the face of everything noble in the world, why did he pen this incident down in his autobiography, immortalizing his act of shame for eternity? Why did he not worry about disillusioning his ardent followers, who would read the book out of their unbounded love for him? Maybe the Mahatma knew that some confessions have the power to sanctify one's soul.

My video titled 'I Am the Change' went viral in February 2017. The idea it sought to push was that 'every girl is your responsibility and not your opportunity'. The ceaseless acts of violence we were witnessing against women spurred me to create the video. 'I Am the Change' was based on the day my Amma chanced upon me, a student of Class Five then, secretly watching the fashion channel, FTV. After confiscating the remote control, she pulled up a chair for herself and sat by my side. She asked me to take a look at the TV screen. To fake embarrassment, I hid my face in my palms. Forcing my hands off my face, Amma said sternly, 'Look at the TV now. Let us find out what you were watching so sneakily.' She pinned me with an unwavering gaze and continued, 'Their bodies only have what your mother has!' Years later, I still can't fathom how unbelievably loaded that small sentence felt. I remember my mind flinching from a whiplash of shame. A few seconds, which felt like an eternity, passed. Then Amma affectionately lifted my face. Gently, she went on to tell me a few things, the crux of which was that while it was natural to be attracted to women, the dignity with which one handles that attraction distinguishes a gentleman.

When my video went viral, the media too reported on it, with the headline, 'Their bodies only have what your mother has—the youngster's video goes viral'. They discussed it and dissected it. The name 'Joseph Annamkutty Jose' also got noticed in conjunction with the video. The son who adopted his mother's name quickly became the talk of the town as people couldn't stop praising his love. Subsequently, I did a few more videos, all of which went viral. Everyone said it was incredibly lucky for a mother to have raised a son who could drive social shifts by openly sharing his acts of glory and shame with the world.

The many comments posted under the video left me baffled. 'A lucky mother.' 'Finally, here's a son who really loves his mother.'

'I wish I had a son who thinks like you.' Doting mothers' affection flooded in through social media.

I wanted to scream my disagreement and frustration at these takes. I wanted to tell them that my mother was not all that lucky to have me as her son and that I did not love her as much as the world seemed to assume I did. But I could not. The admiration the world showered on me splashed hard on the umbrella of truth my conscience had unfurled. At that crossroads of conflict, I found inspiration in the great man Gandhi to confess some truths.

Before we go any further, let me place a humongous piece of irony on the table. The worst opinion I have ever heard about myself—in all my life—had come from my mother. 'Joseph, in this whole wide world, do you know who is the one person with whom I am most guarded while talking? It is you. Out of my three children, it is only with you that I gauge every word I utter. To be honest, I am scared of you.'

That's the reality of what the perfect son prototype's mother really thought about him.

I ponder what made my mother say this about me. God, where did I go wrong? For days, the question bothered me like an itch that I couldn't scratch. The universally accepted theory of sons sharing a deep bond with their mothers has always fallen flat with us. Love felt much more unrestrained between my father and me.

My mother retired as a schoolteacher of excellent repute. Since the day she married my dad, to date, she has managed an efficient home; she is a woman who toils hard. But strangely, when it came to seeking motherly love and affection, I time and again turned to my father. My life sought the warmth he radiated like one of those riverside trees leaning towards the sun. On a hot day, when I started to walk to the bus stop, Appan would immediately say, 'Isn't the sun blazing! Why don't you take the car to the office?' But before that voice of affection could bring a smile to my face, Amma would say, 'If he has no problem taking a bus to his office, let him do that. Why are you compelling him to take the car?'

The office was 40 kilometres away and using the car meant burning Rs 500 on petrol. Was that necessary? Was a youngster—in his prime—walking just under a kilometre on a hot day a portrait of hardship? No. Why was the luxury of an air-conditioned car necessary when a bus was far more economical? Amma's thinking was downright practical, always. But it was Appan's lenient, loving heart that I appreciated more than Amma's foot-firmly-on-the-ground practicality.

In our home, Amma never shied away from voicing her opinions. If anything, her voice was heard above the rest of ours. However, having been on the receiving end of her severe words and scorching temper innumerable times, I was always more receptive to my father's quieter ways of disagreement. The bruises her words had inflicted on my mind over the years had left it numb and inert towards her.

I remember one incident. When I finally realized that a career in sales and marketing would not make me happy, I decided to quit my job. I felt strongly that my path lay elsewhere. For my classic middle-class home, leaving a well-paying job was selfish and stupid, if not suicidal. Every family member needed to be employed to ensure our security. Any deviation from the accepted 9 to 5 was scary. 'Please don't let us down, son,' Amma wept when I told her my decision. Her tears didn't move me an inch. In contrast, Appan's reassuring words and trust in my decision touched me. 'If you are unable to carry on there, you leave it. But we need to find an alternative as soon as possible. We all are by your side. Okay?' He smiled. I went into my room, latched the door, and cried.

Amma doesn't know that I dreaded our conversations as much as, or even more, than she did. It is just that I have never explicitly admitted to it. While I find conveying my ideas to utter strangers easy, I pathetically fail at explaining anything to her routinely. I remember telling Chettan in a moment of utter frustration, 'Our Amma will argue even with God.'

Inside church confessionals, the sin I have repeatedly confessed was losing my temper with my parents. I only ever meant one parent, Amma. Lately, I have been deeply introspective about the two-person country that Amma and I inhabited, where conflicts never ended. Why do I get mad at Amma? Could the fault be mine? Why does Amma always talk so loudly? Despite all my efforts, why does she fail to understand me? Who should change? Me? Amma? Or 'us'?

I made a conscious effort to understand Amma better and correct myself in case I was in the wrong. I started recounting all my memories that involved Amma, one by one. I sought to see her as an individual, wiping aside the conditioning that blinds a son when viewing his mother. For the first time, I decided to look at the world through her eyes, not mine.

Much before she was my Amma, she was a girl who was pushed into marriage at the age of eighteen. She had nothing against her groom to be; she barely knew him. She just wasn't ready for marriage. So, even though her groom was a fair and dashing young man, it was with a heavy heart that she walked into her marital home.

The traditional matrices of beauty did not include her. Amma was a very average-looking girl with a complexion that was nowhere near fair. The world has seldom been fair to 'not so fair' girls. In her new home, a volley of unkind, insensitive and borderline cruel comments awaited the young bride. 'For my looks, I could have gotten fairer girls,' her husband would joke. She overheard obscene remarks that her mother-in-law made about her. 'If you sleep with her, you will have to bathe a hundred times in Kanjoor River to wash the soot off,' the lady told her son. She braved all that but still had to spend most of her honeymoon period alone as her husband was a man who had dedicated his life to social work. The awareness that raising a family down the line would require the income of two people was already firming up in her. That knowledge made it impossible for her to confine herself to managing the household and raising children. She chose to hand her one-year-old son over to her mother to get trained to be a teacher. Needless to say, she was criticized through that entire period. It was only because of her unbendable conviction and tenacious work ethic that she managed to reach her goal, despite the resistance she faced. In short, the initial years of her marriage felt like she was swimming upstream against hardships, while not choking down on sorrows and neglect.

Most of my memories of my mother have her working incessantly, always doing something or the other. She used to wake up before the birds in the morning, sweep the yard, cook breakfast, and pack lunch for her husband and children. Her morning chores meant that she invariably reached her school panting, attempting to outrun the old pendulum clock on the staffroom wall. She used to be a biology teacher. After straining her vocal cords in noisy classrooms, she rushed home after school hours. Her day was hardly done. As soon as she reached home, she would make tea and snacks, do the dishes, clean the house and surroundings, and wash all our clothes. She did all this, decade after decade, like an animal pulling a loaded cart. Tirelessly. Or was she tired? None of us really asked, but there was never a maid at home once we all started going to school.

I have never seen anything out of place in our house. Amma would constantly repeat, 'A place for everything and everything in its place.' Day-old newspapers on the table, cobwebs and dusty ceiling fans were all sights we could never see at home. She had a set of rules for our home and life.

'Keep everything back in the place you picked it from.'

'Be it outside or in your own house, always keep the toilet clean after you use it. It amounts to respecting the person who comes after you. Never leave your mess for another to clean.'

'Never forget a hand that slapped you and a hand that helped you.'

'I don't believe in pretentious prayers done for the sake of rituals; action is my spirituality. I am a "Minimum Christian".'

She was always present, working tirelessly backstage. She never left us lacking in anything. So, of course, I had taken her for granted.

Once, when Amma went away for a month to visit my elder brother in Dubai, Appan 'took charge' of the household chores. Three days in, he folded. 'Joseph, we must really salute her for doing all this single-handedly! My back is already breaking!' he exclaimed. In the forty long years of juggling the household chores and her teaching job, hadn't Amma ever felt that her back was breaking? Had she ever told us so? She must have, many times. It is just that none of us heard her.

Once I start looking for memories of Amma, they keep on coming. Appan's mother had been living with his younger brother for years. 'I would like to bring Mother here and nurse her for some time. I strongly wish to do so,' Amma once told Appan. This thought would have never crossed Appan's mind. We should not forget that in her youth, the old woman was a bully who had harassed and hurt my mother a lot. Remember the mother-in-law who was worried that her son's wife would rub off her dark skin on him? Yes, that same one. Amma and I went together, and brought Ammuma home. Amma took care of that elderly lady with utmost care, compassion and grace. Amma fed, bathed and washed her the entire time she lived with us. I remember another of Appan's brothers saying, 'Heaven is yours, Ettaththi. You could not have done a nobler thing.'

Amma was not just a loud voice in whose wake all our opinions fell mute. She was also a young girl who had fought battles she hadn't picked and still emerged victorious, bruised but brave. She was also a woman who found it in her to forgive and even love a lady who fired shots at a new bride's self-esteem instead of welcoming her into her son's life. A lifetime with her husband and three sons may have roughened her up a little on the outside. Regardless of what anyone thought, felt or understood about Amma, in reality, she was an assortment of all those singularities. She still is and will probably remain so forever.

She craved for her third child to be a girl, and awaited the child's arrival with baby bangles and tiny skirts ready. By now, you should have guessed who came out as her third child: Me—the only one she was scared to talk to, among her three children.

I swell with guilt and struggle in repentance. Amma's short temper and loud voice were just immutable echoes of the screaming scars that life had painted on her. My heart accuses me of never having tried to understand Amma. If I had, I would have been a little more considerate towards her, and maybe gotten the kind of love and affection from her that I had craved for so long.

What we call love is the sum of all these seemingly little things that Amma did. The kind of love that is ever present, so that we recognize it only when it is lost. Now, my conscience corrects me, 'Your mother does have the right to argue even with God.' The occasional sharpness of her words is simply the truth glinting off her heart's chipped edges. The cracks under her feet are journals from the tightrope of life she walked.

My Amma deserves much love! As her son, the least I can do for her is accept her the way she is. I want to think of something other than Amma going through these lines. What would she be thinking? Once she completes reading this chapter, what would she want to tell me?

Would she get teary, yet feel a surge of relief? Amma, I was crying while I wrote this chapter. You are still not the person I love most, but you are definitely the person I respect the most in this whole wide world—and my love for you has increased manifold.

Dear Amma, a thousand kisses on every wound life has inflicted on your heart.

THE WATCHMAN OF LIFE

'We make a living by what we get. We make a life by what we give.'

—WINSTON CHURCHILL

Sister Romula told us to pray to the guardian angel every day before we go to sleep. It is believed that God has appointed a guardian angel to help you when you are in danger. The guardian angel comes to your rescue when you are defenceless, without you having to ask. As a child, I always wished to see those winged angels. But having grown up, I realize that their wings are their hearts and that they have human forms. I realize that … not all angels fly.

On one Sunday, my only day off from work, I received a call from my colleague, Mehul. He said, 'Hey, Joseph, listen. Actor Aju Varghese has agreed to come to the studio to promote their new movie *Goodalochana*. Could you please come in and do the interview?' My first response was anger. Sethu was away visiting his mother. Nilja was in her native village. Martin and Parvathi were just newbies. I realized that as the only RJ (radio jockey) available, I had no choice but to go. Sleep still hovered around my eyelids struggling to decide whether to stay or leave. But I knew that, like me, it too must leave soon. I showered, dressed, got into my car and shot straight to the studio. While driving, every wheel in my mind turned as fast as it could to arrive at the right questions to ask the actor. I didn't know much about the upcoming movie that he and his team were promoting. And as much as I appreciated the opportunity to meet Aju Varghese in person, I knew I would have enjoyed a relaxing Sunday much more.

There was another thing: It had been some time since I had started receiving inquiries about the delay in my next book's arrival. Friends, Facebook friends, family and well-wishers, unconnected groups of people, had come together like a makeshift mob to interrogate me about my writing progress. That Sunday was when I could move my pen enough to report some added pages of solace to them. And it is the same vital Sunday that Aju Varghese has set out to steal.

Aju Varghese reached the studio half an hour after me. When I introduced myself, he said, 'I know you, Joseph. My wife is a fan of yours. She showed me some videos of your talks, which made me kind of a fan too. The things you say are good!' I was surprised. I wasn't expecting that kind of a hello. That day, our chat for the show went well. We got along like two old friends catching up after a while. After the interview, as we were leaving the studio, I noticed Sunilettan signalling something with his eyes. Sunilettan was the security guard of our office. He wanted a selfie with Aju.

'Why not? We will take as many selfies as you want,' Aju said, happy to oblige.

'It is the first time that a celebrity is standing next to me.' When Sunilettan said this, the innocence in his smile was unmissable.

Aju made his way out, leaving just Sunilettan and me in the office.

'Shall I go and bring some tea for you, sir?' Sunilettan asked.

Maybe that was when I paid proper attention to the man for the first time that day. On weekdays, he wears a white shirt and black trousers, and a cap, as part of his uniform. Since it was a Sunday and the office was empty, he wasn't wearing his uniform or cap. Two-day-old stubble stood out on his face, almost every grey strand gleaming right from its follicle.

'Never mind, Suniletta, you relax. I will be leaving soon. I am working on a book these days. Got to get back home, glue myself to the chair and start writing again.'

'Oh, great, sir, so you are a writer. I used to read a lot back in the days when I was recovering.'

'Recovering? What was the illness?' I asked.

'I was down in a hospital bed for some time, sir; that could be a story in itself.' He smiled.

'Then I am not leaving unless I hear it! Just shoot, Suniletta.'

I could see that he was thinking about what he had just said and whether he should have mentioned it at all.

'I haven't told this to anyone here in the office, sir. You would be the first person to know this,' he started hesitantly.

'Feel free, Suniletta.' I hoped my earnestness would put him at ease.

He still struggled with cold feet, but he managed to start.

> Sir, I am an unblemished communist, the kind which lives to uphold communism. The kind that would go to any extent for the ideology. I have a deep-rooted reason for being so, sir. My father was a petty labourer on a farm. The poverty we lived in those days might be unfathomable for many. If we had three meals a day, it would invariably have unripe jackfruit cooked by my mother, and never for once anything else. It was the same story till my early teens. But then, when I reached Class Seven, the great [E.K.] Nayanar's government introduced free 'kanjiyum payarum' for poverty-stricken farm labourers. When someone gives bread to a starving man, not just the bread but the giver will also be looked at with great love. That is when I first heard of the Communist Party. That year, the first unit of SFI

[Student's Federation of India] was established in Vandiperiyar and I became a member of it. When I reached Class Eight, I was elected as the unit secretary. From then, my life was synonymous with the party. It was everything to me. I have even been to jail for a week. Not that I had hurt somebody or wronged anyone, the party instructed me and I obeyed.

We used to engage in a lot of social work under the party's leadership. We collected money to build houses for the homeless, organized blood donation camps and more. One fine day, a friend from the party told me that his friend needed a kidney and asked if I could help find a donor. At that time, I didn't know much about kidney donation. All I knew was that if it was for the party, I would help, no matter what. Right there, I said that I was willing to be the donor. I was told that not just anyone can be a donor and that numerous tests must be conducted before a candidate is selected. I expressed my willingness to undergo the tests as well.

By then, I was already married and had two lovely children. But having said that, even they came second, after the Communist Party. Was I right or wrong about that mindset? I still don't know. The patient who needed the kidney was an elderly man. It turned out that I was a match and could donate a kidney. But before we could proceed any further, the old man died.

Life went on, and one day, we were at a blood donation camp organized by the party. While waiting among the donors, I noticed a young girl with her father. I handed them the programme pamphlets, and elaborated on the camp and the party's humanitarian activities. Before I could finish, the elderly father took hold of both my hands. When he looked at me, pain flickered in his eyes. His daughter's kidney was malfunctioning, and receiving a kidney from a donor was her only chance at living a healthy and peaceful life. To add to the agony, the family was financially weak. When he said he didn't know what to do, he struggled and his voice cracked.

I sat him down. I told him that I had once almost donated my kidney. He was still holding the pamphlet I had given him earlier. I took the pamphlet from his hand, turned it over, placed it on a shaky wooden stool, and holding it firm with my left arm, wrote my phone number on the blank side of it before giving it back to him.

'I am willing. Maybe I couldn't donate back then because I was destined to help you. Please let me know what you decide,' I told him.

That frail man appeared visibly surprised; he couldn't say anything. However, as they were leaving, I gazed into his weak eyes and saw hope in them.

Days went by and, one morning, I received a phone call. The girl's father informed me that he had gathered the necessary funds for the surgery. He requested that I visit the hospital for some tests, and I happily agreed. After undergoing all the required check-ups at the hospital, I was declared fit to be a donor once again. After that, the doctor summoned me. When he spoke to me with authority and clarity for the first time, I heard about the intricacies of organ donation. The last time around, the proposed recipient had passed away by the time I had undergone the basic tests, so I never had a detailed conversation with the doctor.

I'll never forget that day when I understood the gravity of what I was about to do. The sacrifices I would have to make—months in bed, no strenuous activities and long-term medication. I knew I could live with just one kidney, but the rest of the information was a lot to take in. When I imagined a situation where that kidney starts malfunctioning and me, in turn, having to run for a donor, it was unnerving. My mind and body started quivering; my thoughts frightened me. I felt enraged at the kind of stupidity I had displayed when I signed up to become a donor.

I am the sole wage earner in my family; I was a construction worker back then. Who will care for my family if I am hospitalized? What kind of work can I do after this? Questions piled up high in my head, ready to collapse on my soul and crush it.

After leaving the hospital, I headed straight home. The moment I saw my wife and children, I decided to retract my decision. However, the faces of the father and daughter kept flashing in front of me. I shouldn't have given them hope. A sense of guilt began to weigh on my conscience, which I tried countering with logic. While contrasting emotions grappled inside me, my phone rang again, displaying the old man's number. Determined to inform him of my change of heart, I answered the call. However, it was the girl who spoke.

'Uncle, I am going to get admitted tomorrow. I have no words to thank you, uncle. You are an angel sent by God.' Having said this to me, she handed over the call to her father.

'I can only cover the cost of the surgery right now, but I promise to find a way to come up with the rest of the money. Just let me know how much you need and I'll arrange it one way or another. Seeing my daughter smile after a long time means more than anything else to me,' the old man said.

Before hanging up, he didn't even once confirm that I would be available for donation the next day—not even once. That kind of trust left my tongue tied. I just sat in my room alone. I realized that sometimes, every passing second feels heavy on your existence. I felt torn. On one hand, there was my family and our simple life; on the other, there was my promise and the fragile man's last hope for his daughter's painless existence. I concluded that if one is sure that what they are doing is right, one need not calculate much.

'Reach the hospital tomorrow, be assured I will be there too.' I called them and said just that.

How did I manage to make that decision? I don't have an answer to this day.

My wife opposed my decision. I can still see the tears in her eyes and feel the tremor in her speech. She begged me to refrain from destroying our cherished little world. Relatives and friends couldn't hide their resentment as they blamed my decision on nothing but "party fanaticism". Little did they realize that all I had on my mind were the faces of that father and daughter. I stuck to my decision.

The following day, I kept my promise and got admitted to the hospital. A few relatives of the girl visited me and inquired about how much I was expecting. Despite being advised by my family to ask for a significant sum, I once again disappointed them by making another problematic decision that caused more pain.

'Please take care of the basic expenses of my house while I am in the hospital. Other than that, I don't want any money. Just make sure to remember this: Promise me that you'll cast your vote for the Communist Party in the next election.'

Sunilettan finished telling me his life story, almost as if awakening from a trance. I hadn't uttered a word. Then, my essential human rationality kicked in.

'Suniletta, please don't see this as insensitivity or disrespect of any kind. But is all of this true? Me, or, for that matter, any commoner, would find it very hard to believe your story. Do you still have any documents regarding the organ donation?' I asked in a single breath, unable to contain my curiosity.

But even before I completed the question, I realized that it was insensitive and disrespectful, regardless of my initial claim about it not being so. Sunilettan just let out a hearty laugh.

'Sir, when I come tomorrow, I shall bring you the certificates signed by the doctors of Medical Trust Hospital. I'm unsure, but I may have the soft copies on my mobile as well. If so, I shall forward those to you today, sir.'

After some searching, he found the documents on his phone and showed them all to me. It was true. Everything Sunilettan had told me was absolutely true.

After his hospital stay, Sunilettan was bedridden for a while. His wife took on any job she could find to support the family. When Sunilettan finally returned to work, he knew he couldn't go back to his old construction work, so he took up the watchman job.

'This tall, slender man, who greeted me with a smile every day when I arrived at the office, seemed to have a heart bigger than most of us—a colossal one,' I recall thinking at that moment. Without taking a single penny, this watchman gave a part of his body, risking his whole future, and stood guard for a little girl's life. Have you ever felt your eyes moisten out of sheer respect? I felt it that day, standing in front of that man.

In his renowned novel *Goat Days*, Benyamin writes, 'The lives we don't experience are just fabricated stories for us.'

Even as you read this, Sunilettan's story may sound like something I concocted to add drama to my book. In this era, where the norm seems to be to make money even through treachery, in this society that proclaims that not even an eagle flies higher than money, here is a man! Standing at an office door with an undefeatable smile, he tells the world, 'Indeed, there is something that soars above money—and that is humanity.'

This man is not made-up; he is a reality with whom I was fortunate to cross paths.

Oh, watchman of life, the noblest of salutes to you!

FEMINICHI: AN ARMOUR OF SCARS

'I raise my voice not so I can shout but because those without a voice can be heard. We cannot succeed when half of us is held back.'

—MALALA YOUSAFZAI

There was a time in our land's history when women faced the unjust obligation of paying taxes solely for the right to cover their breasts. Nangeli, a woman with unmatched courage, chopped off her breasts, placed them on a plantain leaf, and presented them instead of her taxes. By paying the price with her life, she defied the inhumane tax and the very root of an oppressive ideology behind it. The first bold feminist. Even at that time, there were probably men and women who said, 'Look at her arrogance' or 'Whose loss was it? Only hers and her family's.'

A friend of mine recently shared an experience from her office. Her manager would keep on sending vulgar texts to her. She took screenshots and ensured she had solid proof of his actions before finally meeting him in his cabin. 'I have enough evidence to put you behind bars. The only thing stopping me is the innocent faces of your wife and children that I saw when they visited the office once,' she told him before submitting her resignation. The man stood up and apologized with folded hands.

'Scream', an on-air campaign spearheaded by RJ Nilja, was one of the biggest initiatives undertaken by Radio Mirchi during my first month working there. An incident during a train journey impelled her to take up the initiative. She was sitting in the window seat of a train, as unsuspecting as any passenger enjoying a good view. The train had started moving slowly from a particular station when, through the open window, charged in a hand which squeezed her breast and withdrew! Even though momentarily frozen, she regained her composure quickly, pulled the chain and brought the train to a halt. Nilja leaped out of the wagon's door and began pursuing the assailant through the platform, screaming all the way. While running, she continued to shout that the man had groped her. Some onlookers rushed to help her and caught hold of the culprit, who was then taken away by the Railway Police. In such a scenario, her voice came to Nilja's rescue. The campaign 'Mirchi Scream' aimed to highlight that when attacks on women are increasing, her primary defence should be her ability to raise her voice. As part of the campaign, I also created an awareness video.

Three days after posting that video, I received a message in my Facebook inbox.

'Screaming is useless, and a voice is in vain unless there are ears willing to hear and hearts willing to react,' read the first line of that message. Voice clips, five-, three- and eight-minute long, followed. What those voice clips said were experiences that, to say the least, tormented my mind. Let me share what she said in those voice clips:

> I was in Class Ten back then. My father and mother lived under the same roof but never spoke to each other. Our home was an example of two respected families coming together through marriage, while the individuals getting married begin to lose out

on many things. My parents kept up appearances for the sake of society. My love for them was equal and impartial. So was my rage. Most of their arguments had me at the centre. With whom should I go shopping, who will participate in the school meeting, and what dress should I wear for a particular function? They could ignite fights out of thin air with me as a phantom catalyst.

One day, Achan asked me to accompany him to a function. A colleague of his was hosting a birthday party for their child. I was happy to tag along, wearing the new dress that Achan had bought me a week ago. There were other girls of my age at the party. But, for some reason, I preferred to stick by Achan's side, holding his little finger. Achan encouraged me to mingle with the girls, but I chose to stay by his side. More than once, I noticed Achan's friends gesturing to him from the staircase. It didn't take much thought to realize that it was an invitation for him to join them for a drink. I wrapped my arm around his and pleaded with him not to go.

'I won't drink, molei, but I just have to go and spend some time in their company. It is just a courtesy. I won't drink.' Saying this, Achan asked me to be with the other girls. I still held on to his arm.

'Not more than ten minutes, molei,' Achan said as he left, prising my arm away from his.

Kids were playing everywhere and the music was deafening. I walked over to a corner where other girls my age had gathered, huddled and chatting. Unlike me, it seemed like most of them were already friends, or at least well acquainted with one another. Maybe that's why I felt left out, even though I tried to join their conversations. I didn't want to feel like an unwelcome presence, so I decided to wait in a nearby room until Achan returned. The room was empty, with the lights off, but it felt more comfortable than the loud music and disinterested group of girls outside. I sat on the bed. Even though the room was unlit, I could see the lights outside through the half-open door. I could still see the kids frolicking.

Out of nowhere, a man charged into the room. Alarmed by his unexpected entry, I let out an involuntary shriek. He had assumed the room was empty and was startled. After switching on the lights, he instantly apologized.

'Sorry, molei, Uncle was unaware you were sitting here. I came to use the washroom. Why are you sitting here alone in the dark?' he asked with a lot of affection. He worked with my Achan. I remember seeing him when I visited their office with Achan once.

'I am waiting for Achan; he is upstairs.'

'Amma did not come along?'

'No,'

'Okay, is it fine if Uncle uses the bathroom? And Uncle shall turn the light back off as you don't like it,' he said before walking into the bathroom. He also half closed the door, as it was before he opened it. He went inside the washroom and came out after a while.

I saw his silhouette in the dim light that oozed out of the washroom. I went cold. The man had come out completely naked. I turned my face away out of sheer fear. I realized that I could not move except for the tremor I could feel in my viscera. The only parts of me that succeeded in moving were my eyelids; I shut them tight and literally froze. I could feel him walking close; he sat by my side.

I heard him say, 'Uncle shall be with you till Achan comes', in the same affectionate tone. I objected and tried to move. He instantly got up and latched the door shut.

'Uncle, please let me go to Achan,' I cried. I implored him. I begged.

I was brutally raped. I couldn't even understand what he was doing to me. I writhed in agony. The excruciating pain made me scream aloud. I called out to Achan with all the strength I could muster. My loudest cries for help got drowned in the louder music outside that closed door. If I uttered a word to anyone, he would fire Achan from the office, he threatened me. He sounded like a wild carnivore when he said that.

I washed the blood stains off. I walked out of the room. I could feel a burning revulsion in every cell of my body. Making a futile attempt to control my tears, I rushed upstairs, looking for Achan. I found him there, merrily inebriated. Achan smiled at me, unable to even make out that I was weeping, that I was bleeding. I demanded he hand over the key to our scooter, and he didn't even bother to ask why I needed it. 'Here you go, molei.' He gave it to me after struggling to take it out from his trouser pocket. Currency notes fell out and coins splattered on the floor when the key made its way out of the pocket; Achan didn't notice that either. I ran out of that building.

I didn't know what to do. The place was near Amma's ancestral home. I knew how to ride a two-wheeler only to the extent of what taking rounds on Achan's scooter in our house courtyard had taught me. I got on the scooter and turned on the ignition. My body ached, head to toe. I turned the throttle, stifling an upsurge of emotions. Carrying my deranged self, the vehicle rode itself out of that compound.

While on that scooter, minutes moved as mechanically as they do in reality, devoid of the ornamentations we usually garnish them with, like the ticking of an old watch someone abandoned in a graveyard. The gates of our ancestral home were wide open as if accustomed to welcoming the wounded with open arms. Seeing me enter the courtyard on Achan's two-wheeler, weeping and ruffled, my Maaman rushed towards me in alarm, his arms on his head. The vehicle raced straight ahead to hit a big flower pot and I flew off it, falling unconscious in front of that old, proud house.

While carrying me inside, Maaman and Amma noticed the bruises on me; they assumed it was from the fall they had just witnessed. They told me it was okay. I didn't dare to tell them the truth. I felt like my heart was going to implode, but I still couldn't speak. I was afraid because the man had threatened to fire Achan and I was terrified my father would roam around jobless.

I went into depression in the years that followed. Darkness petrified me. So did men. Eventually, my parents separated. Since then, I lived with my mother. When I matured over the years, I told my mother what had happened to me. My mother didn't shed a single tear. She held me close, firmly. She told me that I had not lost anything. She told me that this world also has men who love and respect women as they should be. Witnessing my mother, a lady who lived with utmost dignity and courage, all by herself helps me grow. When she introduced me to yoga classes, enrolled me in dance training, and stood by me for every wish of mine, she continued to teach me the glory in the pride of a woman who lives anchored to her indomitable spirit.

Today, I run yoga and dance classes for girls. I am writing a beautiful story with the blood that had spilled out of an old wound. It has long lost its power to hurt me. But still, when newspapers deliver accounts of violations meted out on women, when movies objectify a woman's body brazenly, when an unidentifiable perverted remark spikes out from a crowd of men, even today, a few droplets of fresh blood seem to trickle down from those old gashes. And this is not just my story; it is the story of millions.

Today, society calls people like me 'Feminichi'. But time will make them realize that the cause compelling me to be a Feminichi, unapologetically so, protects their mothers, sisters and daughters.

Feminism is the voice that speaks for the women who were, are and unfortunately will continue to be silenced. Feminism is

> not hatred for men, not a war for gender equality; it is not an attempt at female glorification. It is the name given to a voice that urges women to live with self-respect and independence.
>
> So, Joseph, returning to the on-air campaign on your radio channel, I want to say this respectfully. What we need are not campaigns that teach women to scream but campaigns that teach men to conduct themselves in a way that no unfortunate woman ever has to scream. Yes, brother, I am what they call a Feminichi. But not a Feminichi who hates all men, but one who was forced to endorse that tag by some men.

Her words came from the depth of conviction and experiences. The rest of this chapter is for the male friends reading this page.

There is a feminist inside every wounded woman. When a woman stands up for the rights of women, the world and history have witnessed her getting pejoratively labelled as 'Feminazi' or a 'libber'. Now, those labels are beginning to find their domestic derivatives in derogatory terms like 'Feminichi'. It is unfair to misconstrue their self-respect as arrogance. Because they survived gender-based violations simply for being born female. What do we men know about that anguish?

I recommend searching for 'Nadia Murad' online if you have the time. She won the Nobel Peace Prize in 2018. Her life story has been published under the title *The Last Girl*. If you can, I suggest reading it. She escaped from the sexual slavery of ISIS terrorists and bravely spoke out against them. She continued to fight against activities that victimized or exploited females.

Type 'CNN Heroes—Anuradha Koirala' in your YouTube search bar. Check out the first video that comes up. You will see a lady in her seventies who has managed to save more than 10,000 young girls from sex trafficking. She didn't just rescue them but also helped them understand that life hasn't slipped away from them. She taught them how to live it well.

What could be worse than cries that go unheard? According to statistics released by the National Crime Records Bureau (NCRB) in 2016, the percentage of minor females subjected to sexual assaults has risen to an alarming 82 per cent. Most shockingly, 95 per cent of the assaulters are family members, close relatives or neighbours.

If you can gather the courage needed for an open conversation, ask your mother, 'Mom, did you go through any difficult experiences when you were young?' Ask your sister, 'Have you ever faced any sexual threats on the streets, in public transportation, or from anyone in our family and social circle?'

When an eight-year-old girl was raped and killed in a temple in Kashmir, the whole country stood up in remonstration. I shall wind up this chapter with the words I remember seeing in the hands of one of the protestors.

'What if you are the next?'

Men may need to add more to that question and ask themselves.

What if your mother is next?

What if your sister is next?

What if your wife is next?

What if your child is next?

IN THE RIGHT SPIRIT

'I am not going to change the world, and you are not going to change the world, but we can help. We can all help.'

—CRISTIANO RONALDO

Cristiano Ronaldo has one of the most extensive fan bases among all athletes globally. He was chosen as the celebrity ambassador for the blood donation campaign called BE THE 1. He donates blood twice a year and, to maintain his eligibility for the same, CR7 (Cristiano Ronaldo, jersey number 7, as his fans call him) has decided to refrain from consuming alcohol and getting tattoos. This may be one reason why he has a large number of fans off the field as well. He once wrote on his Facebook page, 'When we donate blood, we save someone's life. How great a thing is that?'

'How boring is this life! Every single day feels like a clone of the rest. A change is indispensable,' I thought, probably, like many others who were thinking the same thought around the time. Outside, the rain poured down with some kind of nasty vengeance, and the day ahead looked drenched. As I stood staring at the rain out of my office window, a shower of sheer monotony was soaking my mind.

The phone in my cabin rang, cutting through my contemplation. I picked it up.

'Joseph, are you A+? One of my cousins is at Lakeshore Hospital and he needs blood,' Biju sir from the IT team asked on the other end.

'I am A+! But since it's Monday morning, I must talk to my boss. If he allows it, I shall come.' I went straight to Jinoj's cabin.

'But where do you hide so much blood!' Jinoj gave me permission, but not before taking a good-humoured dig at my skinniness at that time.

The car with Biju sir and me irreverently sliced through the rain pouring down. Biju sir began to tell me about the patient and the illness.

'The lady is fifty-five years old and has bone marrow cancer. A bone marrow transplant is the solution. The surgery will take place at Aster Medicity, and this will be the very first bone marrow transplant to take place there. The patient has been admitted there for the past three months.'

'In that case, why are we going to Lakeshore Hospital?' I asked.

'Joseph, I was about to tell you. The patient requires platelets, not whole blood. After a bone marrow transplant, the patient must receive blood platelets from a healthy donor to enable the body to produce healthy blood independently. If this is successful, it can greatly reduce the likelihood of the cancer returning. However, even a small error in the blood analysis can be fatal for the patient. A person will be accepted as a donor only after utmost scrutiny. If we get approval from Lakeshore Hospital, the donation will happen at Aster Medicity two days later.'

We reached the hospital.

'He has come to donate platelets for the case at Aster.' Biju sir introduced me to the nurse.

'I hope at least this one works. We need good veins on both hands. You are the fifth person today; all the four before you failed to pass.

You look underweight, though. This involves taking three litres of blood from the body. Anyway, let us try. Come along!' the nurse said in a casual, matter-of-fact tone.

'Three litres of blood?' I started to feel fear breathing down my neck. It was the first time I had heard about platelet donation. That day, I realized boredom leapt and vanished into the bushes when fear approached.

'Let's see if you have good veins on both hands,' the nurse said, tying a string tightly around my arms. Considering how tightly she was tying it, I wanted to ask her if she was trying to make just a vein pop out or my other internal organs too. But before that happened, I saw my vein surfacing.

'We found it,' she exclaimed, her voice brimming with excitement. Her elation reminded me of our reaction as little school boys when we stumbled upon long-lost cricket balls in the bushes near the ground.

With the form that the donor needed to fill out in her hand, she started asking me questions. Aloud.

'When did you last donate blood?'

'Five months ago.'

'Did a dog bite you recently?'

'No, sister!' I couldn't resist a giggle because I found that question funny. Little did I know there were more loaded ones lined up.

'Did you have sexual intercourse with strangers?'

'No.'

'How about animals?'

These questions may appear simple when answering them with check marks on paper. However, when asked directly, even the most basic responses can be as challenging as spelling floccinaucinihilipilification.

The nurse proclaimed that I was eligible to donate platelets. As I left the room, I found the patient's husband waiting outside. He appeared to be around fifty years old, with signs of sleep deprivation stagnating in his tired eyes. Holding rosary beads and sporting a days-old grey stubble on his face, he seemed worn out and weary.

'Son, thank you. For the next week, we will need half a litre of platelets daily. Today is the fourth day, and with God's grace, we have managed to find donors for the next two days. You need to go to Aster Medicity after two days, son—'

Before the man could finish, the doctor beckoned us to his room. He sat us down and started explaining the process.

'Platelet donation will take around three hours, Joseph. Blood from one of your hands will be sent into a machine. After extracting platelets from the blood, the machine will pump it back into your body. Half a litre of platelets is the volume we seek from a person; three litres of blood will have to travel through the machine.'

I slowly began to realize that this would not be the usual blood donation experience I was used to. It felt more serious and complicated. Was I walking into a trap? I shouldn't have come; a part of my mind condemned me.

'I thought it was going to be a normal blood donation. But this … I need to think again. Don't take me wrong,' I began, suspicion lacing my tone.

'Oh God, please, son! Please don't say so! It is after so many hardships that we managed to find a donor. We are still short of two people. We need platelets for a week without any lapse. There is no risk involved for the donor. What is at risk is my wife's life!' The man's hand weakly gripped my arm, his eyes filled with unmistakable fear.

The doctor intervened.

'Joseph, the donor should not have any alcohol in their system; so he should not be a regular drinker. He should be in good health and not have had even a common cold for two whole days before the donation. We need to ensure that he has no cuts or bruises on his body. More than twenty people come here every day wanting to donate and almost all of them get rejected due to the alcohol factor.

Even if all the other conditions are good, we need strong veins for the donation process. You are a perfect candidate for this.'

'Give me five minutes. I have to make a phone call.' I exited the doctor's room and took out my mobile phone to call Amma.

'How did it turn out, brother?' A youngster approached me and asked. I quickly cut the call and turned around.

'How did what turn out?' I asked.

'The check-up, brother. I learnt that you are fit. The patient you will donate to is my mother. You will come, right?' He looked at me as if I were their saviour.

At that moment, Amma called back. I did not pick up her call. I stood there looking at her face shining on my phone's display.

'I will come,' I said to him.

I walked into the doctor's room and conveyed my willingness. I must confess, though, that I didn't do it out of any great goodness. I just felt so; so I did so.

'Good, Joseph. You must take utmost care of yourself for the next two days. Pay attention so that you don't get any cuts on your body; no alcohol, no medications and seven hours of sleep at night. Avoid eating out and drink plenty of water. Remember that these two days, when you are taking care of your life, you are safeguarding another's.' The doctor shook my hand.

Looking back, I realize I took the best care of myself in those two days. I avoided any late-night chats and went to bed early. I took a break from my routine morning game of badminton. I asked Amma to pack food for me so that I could have a nice, home-cooked meal during office hours. I also skipped a dear friend's birthday bash. None of those compromises were as easy in practice as writing them down here is. Or could it be that when the benefactor is a complete stranger, even the small sacrifices we make—if we can call them sacrifices at all—begin to seem mammoth?

Two days later, I reached Aster Medicity. The father and son were waiting for me. I was subjected to a blood check once more. After verifying everything again, two nurses ushered me into another room. I saw a huge machine there. I reckoned that it was the machine that was going to take the platelets off my blood.

'Lie down peacefully. You will need to stay that way for two hours. This machine, this one right here, will function like a part of your body for the next two hours. If you feel any discomfort, let us know. We will be here with you.'

They gave me a few more instructions before they pierced the first needle deep into the vein of my left hand. The needle was bigger than the ones we usually encounter. That needle opened the path for the blood to move from my body to the machine. Following suit, another equally big needle went into my right arm. After extracting the necessary platelets, it would let the blood back into my body.

I lay there for two hours, feeling dizzy, my body going weak at times. When it was over, simply standing up felt difficult. I was given two bottles of juice and a packet of biscuits. After resting for some time, I stood up and slowly walked out. I felt more and more exhausted with every step. Biju sir was waiting for me. As we crossed a few doors, the patient's husband rushed towards me.

'Son, are you alright?' When he held my hands and asked this, I could feel his palms tremble.

'Nothing wrong. I am alright. Got to head straight home.'

'Thank you, son,' he said, pressing my hands to his forehead. I could feel his tears on my skin. I told him that I would remember them in my prayers and I returned home.

Later, I found out that the woman not only survived, but she fully recovered, which made me happy to have been a part of her healing process.

I didn't write thus far to praise or glorify myself. The point I am trying to get across is a much larger one. In the case of this woman, 90 per cent of potential donors were rejected due to alcohol consumption. Over fifty students from her son's college were dismissed because traces of alcohol were found in their bodies. I enjoy a good bottle of beer, but now I realize that when I drink, I miss out on the opportunity to save another person's life. Alcohol can diminish the ability to save someone's life, which is a godly capability.

Lots of poor chaps get trapped when movies project alcoholism as synonymous with heroism and indicative of masculinity. The hero walks into his classroom, taking a few swigs as he enters, his friends celebrating their failure in an exam with a liquor party and the hero's father, who justifies his drunk son. All these look exciting on-screen. But it could be a one-way route to a world of tears in real life.

I am aware that times have changed. The things I am jotting down are probably a bit old school by now. But then, the good, the right and the apt are never old school.

Christiano Ronaldo is the heartthrob for millions of football fans. His father was an alcoholic, and he said that, as a kid, he always fantasized about a great father–son relationship. Ronaldo doesn't drink and he has never been tattooed. He also donates blood multiple times every year. Why do Ronaldo fans fail to see the man beyond his game? Because *that* is a real hero.

In September 2017, Virat Kohli decided to stop endorsing beauty products and soft drinks. Previously, he was the brand ambassador of Fair and Lovely, and Pepsi. His decision to forgo lucrative endorsements was motivated by his concern for the well-being of young people. When he announced his decision, he cited two reasons: First, he stated that soft drinks are unhealthy; and second, he emphasized that beauty is innate, and that individuals should embrace and appreciate their natural appearance.

One of the most memorable responses I've ever received on social media was from an Oscar winner. He won the incomparable recognition for Best Original Score in 2008. I am talking about none other than the great A.R. Rahman! I have a line of his that I've turned into a wall poster in my room. It goes like this: 'I have too many responsibilities and principles. There's no time for "guilty" pleasures.'

I once DMed a picture of this poster to him on Instagram and asked, 'Did you say this, sir?' I still have the screenshot of his reply, 'Yes.' Rahman has dominated the Indian music scene for thirty years. He has been referred to as the 'Mozart of India' and there have been no allegations against him. How many generations have been moved to dance, are entertained and healed by his songs? When George Mallory was asked why he wanted to conquer Mount Everest, he famously replied, 'Because it's there.' The reply illustrated the idea that conquering Mount Everest was a real possibility. Hanging those words of Rahman on my wall was my attempt to keep reminding myself that such principles and discipline are achievable: a possibility.

Future generations need to embrace a new kind of heroism. For many reasons, the examples I have mentioned may not seem as immediately appealing as negative or toxic displays of pseudo-heroism. However, these quieter acts of bravery could lead to substantial and meaningful changes in life. Does the machismo that arises from consuming flavoured spirits make someone a hero? Or should we define a hero as someone who navigates life in the right spirit?

Shouldn't we give that a shot?

THE TREES OF SHADE

'Hope is a good thing, maybe the best of things, and no good thing ever dies.'

—*THE SHAWSHANK REDEMPTION*

Every year, the World Health Organization (WHO) celebrates 7 April as World Health Day. In 2017, the chosen theme for discussion was depression. Statistics show that more than 300 million people suffer from depression. The tagline of the campaign led by the WHO to counter depression was 'Let's Talk'. The best way to overcome this condition is to have a space to open up about one's fears, anxieties and agonies. Life seems to be like a line that the legendary actor Kuthiravattam Pappu says in one hilarious movie scene while narrating his narrow escape from a dangerous road roller accident on a cliff. He says, 'If I had slid a foot to this side or a foot to that side, the engine and I would have become particles and powder!' Without friends and folks I could open up to, 'my engine and I would have become particles and powder' a long time ago. In the context of how sad a state many human beings are in, even referring to that timelessly funny movie scene tastes terrible on my tongue.

I looked at her. Her hair was neatly parted, braided and tied with a bright red ribbon. The rosary thread around her neck seemed fragile, as if it could break any moment. She was a fair, big-eyed tenth-standard student. She sat before me, wearing the green and white school uniform and a bright smile. In the session I conducted earlier that day, she seemed the smartest in the class—active and readily answering my questions. The illuminating smile never left her face for a second; neither did the curiosity in her eyes hide itself when they followed me through my session. I was reluctant when asked to conduct a motivational session for Class Ten students. I told the teacher that I wasn't someone who could lead a class solely because I had written a book.

'This school has many underprivileged students. Your Facebook posts prompted me to invite you. You need to tell them some good stuff like that. They don't heed our words much. But when it comes from a youngster like you, the students may be more receptive. Kindly come,' the teacher persuaded me again. Even though I decided to go, I needed to clarify certain things.

'Teacher, I am not a motivational speaker. I am willing to share things I know, but they may not be precisely what you expect. Easy ways to study, tips and tricks to succeed in life … It will be none of that. I could probably share with them whatever I got from the bit of reading I do and, of course, whatever my own life experiences have taught me.'

'That will do, Joseph. That would be great, thank you.'

Revisiting some books I had read, I envisioned a session that intertwined stories of lives that encountered setbacks but ultimately triumphed—a tiny bundle of those that wouldn't let boredom sneak in.

When I reached the school, its appearance surprised me—unpleasantly, though. Everything about the premises looked dilapidated. In the school grounds, a few kids were playing football. Just one glance at the ball's condition was enough to understand the state of affairs: A heavily damaged football, with its orange bladder exposed instead of concealed. It was the ramshackle ball of a ramshackle school.

Proceeding to the staff room, I was saddened to see the amenities that the teachers thrived on. The washroom had a tattered, empty jute sack as a makeshift floor mat; it had 'Pavizham Palakkadan Matta Rice' written on it. Besides a couple of wobbly chairs, only one piece of furniture was in that room. It was an old, lonely wooden desk with a solemn air about it. Its top was divided by neat lines, made with chalk, and the space between two neighbouring lines indicated the area available for a specific teacher. Yet, their books and fountain pens peacefully shared the desk without territorial conflicts or real estate disputes.

The teacher who had contacted me requesting the session guided me to a not-so-big hall on the building's rickety first floor. The hall's interiors instantly took me back to my own school days, about twenty years ago. The white walls were covered in map-like patterns due to moisture. Natural cracks on the wall paint appeared to intertwine harmoniously with the numerous pen and pencil markings left by generations of children who learnt to write at that school.

On one side, the girls sat on newspaper sheets spread on the floor, while the boys sat on benches.

The teacher introduced me to the class.

'This sir has come to talk with you all. Everyone should listen attentively. And remember, after forty-five minutes, girls and boys should swap seats. So, the boys will sit on the newspapers and girls should sit on the benches.'

I saw joy and curiosity on everyone's faces because a young outsider was about to address them. I started from those smiles.

'Listen, your teacher brought me here to help you become better kids. But you are already doing great, aren't you?' I began.

'Yes!' they chorused cheerfully.

'Can I be honest with you? I came in to chat with you guys for some time, and that's it. What shall we talk about? How about Sachin Tendulkar? Do all of you like Sachin?'

'Yes, we like him!' the class shouted unanimously, not having to think for a moment.

I talked about Sachin, Messi and Malala, punctuating my speech with anecdotes about some remarkable people I had encountered. The class listened attentively to my entire talk. When I finally concluded, the teacher who had invited me spoke to the class.

'If anyone wishes to have a personal conversation with sir, raise your hand. The first three will get the opportunity.'

Among those three students, the first one to raise her hand was the girl sitting in front of me—the one I mentioned at the beginning of this chapter.

'Namaskaaram, sir,' the girl said with a smile, her hands folded. Then she took me aside.

'You don't have to address me as "sir". I noticed you were very active during the session. Come on, go ahead. What is it that you want to talk to me about?'

Grief suddenly spread over her happy face, like grey clouds appearing out of the blue and painting a dark picture over a bright, sunny sky. It took her a few moments before she could start speaking.

'Sir, I'm always crying inside. Today, after a long time, I laughed for a while. I live each day burning within.'

Her eyes started moistening. It didn't take long before she burst into tears.

I said nothing—I let her cry and waited for her to speak again.

'Sir, a senior from a nearby school had feelings for me. He expressed his interest and pursued me persistently. I rejected him multiple times, but he continued to follow me, professing his love and attempting to convince me of his sincerity. Over time, I empathized with him and, eventually, we developed mutual affection. The adoration grew with time. Once, he asked me if we could go somewhere and have tea. I refused saying that if my family came to know, I would be dead meat. But when he continued to plead, I agreed with the condition that it would be the first and last time I took that risk. However, those rides started happening more often … It became a regular habit.'

By the time she reached this point, she started crying again, louder. I could see the other two students waiting to talk to me, watching her from a distance and discussing something between themselves.

I pulled my chair closer to hers and asked her not to cry. Then, I asked her to continue talking. Wiping her eyes, she stared out of the window, clearly lost in thought. After that momentary pause, she continued.

'After that, I went with him wherever he wanted me to. I went solely out of my love for him. However, it turned out that what he loved was just my body. Once he had his fill of it, he discarded me.'

She paused and took a deep breath, exhaling audibly. She struggled to speak, and a few quiet seconds passed at a snail's pace between us.

'Am I an immoral girl, sir?' That is all she managed to articulate.

All the rubbing and wiping had reddened her eyes. Tears of naivety rolled down her cheeks. Her head had drooped in shame. Holding the rosary beads tight to her bosom, she wept.

'My mother is a guileless person. Kneeling, she prays for me every single day of her life. She constantly tells my younger sister to make me her role model. I don't know how long it has been since I ever spoke without restrictions to my mother or sister. I used to be very good at studies. Not anymore. All I live by is guilt.' Her face fell.

'Chetta,' she continued, 'how can a person betray anyone who loves them deeply? I never did anything bad towards him, so why did he have to be pitiless towards me? Could you help me, Chetta? My family would kill me if they found out. I don't have the liberty of being honest to my own people.'

The questions she harboured were those that anyone hurt by love would have had. To get wounded in her body and soul at such a young age was more than what a Class Ten student could possibly bear.

'Every drop of tear you shed reflects your deepest love for your Appan and Amma. Whatever you think has blemished your life, it is not stronger than what virtuous tears can wipe off. You did not do anything wrong, and what is more, there is a lot of goodness in you. Who knows, what if this helps you become better? What if it empowers you to love Appan and Amma more than you already do? If you evolve into a better sister? What if it makes you the best student in your class once again? Your capability for love is still unbroken. This guilt won't do anyone any good. Let me share with you a small line that greatly influenced me: "We can't go back to life and start everything all over again, but we can begin well today so that it will have a beautiful ending." We can't go back to the old life and start over again, can we? But if we start well today, we can give a fantastic finish to this phenomenal game called Life. You still have a month before your exams. Starting today, study hard like you used to before. You should get back to being the best student in the class. When the Class Ten results come out, I will ask your teacher who scored the highest. Make sure the name she gives me is yours!'

A smile shone on her face, like the sun reappearing after a rainstorm. She shut her eyes tightly for a second. Then she stood up and bowed. When she walked out of the room, her stride had a newfound determination to it.

All three students who spoke to me that day had problems that did not suit their age. They all lacked a common factor: Parents they could confide in, who could be understanding and compassionate to their needs.

Maybe their parents were unsophisticated—parents who flipped out if the child went out for tea with someone, parents whose hearts were shallow, who were quick to worry over minor things. For the slightest hint of anything unusual, they felt that their child was violated.

It leaves you with the impression that parents must first be taught what defines an ideal education.

An ideal education should be a combination of intellectual and psychological growth.

To truly nurture a child's intellect, both their mind and brain must develop together. While providing access to top schools, necessary study resources and extra tutoring can enhance brain development, it's also important to consider how to foster the growth of their minds. What exactly do we mean when we talk about the growth of a child's mind?

Being able to cope with happiness and sadness, victories and defeats, or gains and losses with inner calmness—all of these could be signs of maturity. If your teenage son has this kind of mental clarity, he's less likely to attempt suicide just because he didn't get the TV remote when he wanted it. Similarly, your daughter won't be intimidated or silenced by unwanted touches in public; she will speak up and fight back.

The concept of having a mature mindset can be understood through the famous saying, 'Be street-smart, not book-smart.' Street-smart individuals are attuned to the practicalities of life and can identify potential dangers. They can react effectively. These confident, dynamic individuals may not always excel in academics. Book-smart individuals diligently study for good grades and may be very geeky about the curriculum. They are typically obedient and may think that even speaking to your bench-mate while the teacher is teaching is a sin that needs to be confessed. A complete education should enable a child to be both book-smart and street-smart in balanced proportions.

The first step would be to create an atmosphere at home that permits open conversations. If the same parents who picked up the child when she fell, tickled her back to laughter and comforted her with a toy begin lashing out at the slightest mistakes of the child when she is growing up, how can anyone expect that growth be wholesome then? How can their minds grow without feeling restricted?

I still remember an incident that another young girl once told me. Her dad, who happens to be a doctor, took her to a shop, bought a bottle of poison, and threatened her: 'If you are still in love with that lad, your mother and I will end our lives consuming this.' How could that girl be expected to throw away an eight-year-long love affair? The guy she loved was a good, well-educated and soundly employed individual, and he was very eligible in many aspects. However, the girl's father objected simply because he was not a doctor. It seemed like the father expected his daughter to be nothing more than someone enslaved to his wishes.

When you drag your children into the framework of your dreams, have an eye to see their little dreams being stomped upon and crushed. One of the cult films of Malayalam cinema, *Spadikam*, shows how such a father turns his once-good child, Thomas Chacko, into a dreaded goon called Aaduthoma. On the other hand, our nation's history shows how forgiveness from a father towards his son, Mohandas, who confessed his mistakes through a letter, led the young man to transcend into a Mahatma. If you can't forgive the little mistakes of your children, then who possibly can?

What comes to my mind at this moment is the love of my father. While pursuing my MBA, I failed miserably in my mathematics exams. My family had invested Rs 6 lakh in the course. Somewhere along the way, I had gotten lost. When I went to tell my parents, who were esteemed teachers with a long history of guiding thousands of students to victory, of this failure, all I could anticipate was resentment and censure. But instead, my father bought me a masala dosa!

'It is okay; we will try again,' he told me.

From that second, his words carried my life ahead. It was okay; I can try again. What could be more potent than igniting a small flame of hope in the heart of a shattered soul?

Children thrive when they have the reassurance that their home is a safe space for expressing anything and everything. If your children, who are studying abroad, unfortunately end up in trouble, they will confidently return to the safety of their homes on the next flight. They wouldn't consider something stupid or some sort of self-harm if you have successfully implanted in their hearts a picture of you smiling, arms spread wide, standing firm, ever ready to welcome them back. Without some shade trees, people like me would have wilted and left a long time ago. The line separating sanity and depression is getting thinner with time. Still, what keeps that line from breaking is the shade of a boulevard of love that the people around us planted and watered. The biggest problem faced by today's youngsters is the absence of such shades of comfort in their lives. Lacking a friend to turn to when your mind is a mess is a dangerous form of impoverishment.

In the movie *Pranchiyettan*, the saint asks Francis, 'All that we believe we achieved, are those real achievements?'

To support someone seems a worthy goal in life—to be the sheltering greenery of a tree in which someone scorched by life's glaring heat can seek refuge.

'Thank you, God!' That is all I can say today. As I write this, the smiling faces of those who extended a helping hand whenever I stumbled and fell are parading through my mind. My life could have fallen apart at many points if those kind words and extended arms never entered it. They gave me the energy to go on; they were my trees of good shade.

The road of life still extends in front of me, reaching as far as the eye can see, into invisible horizons. I may stumble along the way, but I have no fear. I am protected by the love of my parents, supported by a handful of wonderful friends and by the Lord, who serves the holy supper of love.

And when I remember that my life is an aggregate of the love and kindness of a bunch of people, my eyes can't help but moisten.

I pray now, 'O, Lord, make me a forever tree of shade for someone.'

THE DEMOLITION MAN

'Revenge isn't always sweet, but it can be beautiful.'

—STEPHEN YOSHIMURA, Professor of Communication Studies, University of Montana

In the UEFA Champions League, football matches start after both teams are photographed standing before a board that says, 'Say no to racism.' Racist abuses are unfortunately quite common in football. Many times, we see the crowd shouting 'ape' when the ball is with someone who is not white. During a 2014 match between Barcelona and Villareal, a spectator threw a banana at Dani Alves while he was preparing to take a corner kick. The spectator also made monkey gestures at him. Without hesitating or checking to see who threw it, Dani Alves simply picked up the banana, ate it and took the corner kick. Everyone applauded this dignified and intelligent response, as Dani Alves had turned the tables on the person trying to provoke him.

While driving home, my mind wrestled with one question with all its might.

'Why did they not select me?'

A team from Airtel had visited our campus to recruit fresh postgraduates. The first round, the group discussion, went smoothly for me. The second round, the interview, went almost as well as the first.

The only challenge ahead was to sail through the third round successfully. For a moment, I visualized myself clearing it. Just imagining the goosebumps I would experience began to give me goosebumps. Securing a job, fostering pride at home and earning respect in my neighbourhood … Gosh! I imagined swaggering in front of the teacher who dared to declare once, 'Anyone who employs you must be certified crazy.' The checklist of post-success celebration programmes was big and bulleted. In my mind, I was envisioning this self-directed movie with me also as the lead when I was interrupted by an announcement from our job placement coordinator, Roshan. He called out the names of the candidates selected for the final round, and mine was not among them. My dreams of being employed seemed to be dashed, and I felt disheartened.

So, that movie of personal triumph I had directed in my mind would never be premiered. As I said in the beginning, while I was driving back home, all I could think of was this dream-breaker episode. It was supposed to be a fantastic day, but it turned out to be pathetic. Sad.

The main gate was closed as usual when I reached the compound of my house. I could see Amma plucking tulsi leaves in our front yard. That day, I was a defeated man. I did not even feel like doing my usual round of cacophonous honking. Amma moved in ultra-slow motion and opened the gate for the car to enter.

'Why don't you just honk unnecessarily and piss me off? You know I have just got habituated.' Well, she didn't say so, but I read that in her demeanour. I parked the car on our porch, turned off the ignition and sat inside, resting my forehead on the steering wheel. Perhaps Amma sensed something was wrong. She stood outside the raised car window and I could see a mother's perpetual apprehension building up on her face.

'Why are you not getting out?' She opened the door herself and asked me to get out.

'Amma, I could not make it to the final round. I got ousted,' I said with a sigh.

'Leave it, Joseph. The result of the Kancor interview is still to come, right? You will clear that for sure. Come in; I will make you a cup of tea,' she said, going inside.

I sat on the sofa listlessly and switched on the TV. As I gazed at the screen, I heard the sound of our main gate opening. I walked to the door, curious to see who had come now. When I opened the door, I was shocked by what I saw. The car that I had parked in the porch was moving! It pushed through the unlatched gate and started rolling down the road! 'Amme!' I shrieked involuntarily. Even before I could complete my shriek, our Maruti Swift car, displaying no sign of conscientiousness, demolished our neighbour's compound wall! It proceeded to park itself beneath the shattered wall, positioning itself thus that it blocked the road.

I ran towards it and looked around quickly. No human soul had witnessed what just happened!

'I was just having tea when I heard a crumbling noise. I saw the wall had fallen when I came out to check.' If I could manage that narrative with conviction, no one would have any doubt of my involvement. I did think so. I had my reasons to be confident about that explanation. The compound wall was ancient. 'Why did you take the trouble of sending your car if you wanted me to fall? I would have happily obliged if you had just sneezed aloud!' That is what the wall would have said if it could speak. Yes, the wall was that weak and brittle.

I didn't waste a second. I ran home, grabbed the car keys and quickly returned to the car. I started the engine and parked it inside once again, and this time, I made sure to pull the handbrake up. After that, I glanced at the back of our car. My high hopes came crashing down when I saw what I saw. The rear glass was cracked entirely. The back end, as a whole, resembled the face of a boxer, who got pummelled against the ropes by someone no lesser than Iron Mike Tyson. In many places, the bright white paint had been replaced by the colour of gravel on the wall. In areas where gravel did not coat, large black patches stood out.

I was confident I could tell the story, 'The wall fell by itself', but 'the car got into this shape by itself'? I knew there was no way I could pull that one off.

'How could it have happened, son?' My mother could not hide her disbelief when she saw the car. 'We are lucky that no one was on that road, by God's grace!'

A wall pulled to pieces and a car smashed out of shape—is that what luck and God's grace looked like? My mother made no sense to me. There was only one reason behind the occurrence: I had forgotten to pull the handbrake. It was as clear as daylight, but my ego wasn't letting me admit that.

I had only watched such scenes in movies. The potential disgrace that loomed if anyone discovered the truth seemed an absolute reputation-killer. I decided to go ahead and deal with the scenario, come what may. I met Mary Chechi, my neighbour whose wall I had freshly dismantled, to explain.

'Chechi, your compound wall got slightly demolished. The car somehow left our house on its own. We are ready to compensate for the loss incurred. And I have a request: Try not to tell many people about this utterly unpremeditated development,' I told her.

'The car *left* your house on its own? Are you talking about your car or your wife?' I waited for some response on those sarcastic lines to leap out of Mary Chechi's mouth. But it didn't. I think prudence took over.

'It was an old wall, son. It is okay. We will think about and decide on the compensation. Anyway, you need not worry,' was all Mary Chechi said.

'Appan is out for his walk. You meet him and tell him. But I still can't understand how this could happen; the car went away as if it were cross with us.' My mother was still in shock. 'That is what even I don't understand, Amma.' I acted baffled. I could manage Amma by hiding behind her confusion, but with Appan, I knew the task was challenging, if not impossible.

'Appan has not taken his umbrella with him; he must be standing somewhere. You take an umbrella and go meet him.' Amma was panicky.

I took an umbrella and headed to the ground next to Assisi Shanti Kendra, where Appan usually went on his evening walks. I saw Appan at a distance, along with Varghese Maash, another walker of Appan's walking guild. With the rain and a small umbrella to share, the duo appeared to be slithering towards me as a unit.

'You have a great son. See how he acted according to the situation,' remarked Varghese Maash, seeing me approach with an umbrella for my father.

'It must be her who sent him.' Appan didn't have to think twice. 'Anyway, you may go now, Varghese Maashe, and thank you.' They waved goodbye to each other and parted.

'How was today's interview?' asked Appan.

'Oh, I couldn't go beyond the second round, Appa. But I am confident about the results from the Kancor company.'

'Yes, true. Let what is gone be gone. You cheer up.'

'Appa, there is another thing I want to tell you …'

'What is it?'

I started talking, attempting to sound as casual as possible.

'I still have no idea how something like that could ever happen. I mean, I had parked our car on the porch, went inside and was waiting in our living room as Amma was getting me tea. Appa, you know what happened then? Our car just moved ... All by itself ... And went through the gate onto the road and ended up mildly demolishing Mary Chechi's compound wall. Can you believe it! And ya, there are some light damages, or maybe not so light, to the car's rear end. But nothing to worry about; we have insurance, right Appa?' I managed to conclude as if narrating a strange incident that happened to an unfortunate family on a distant continent.

Appan said nothing; he looked at me with a naughty grin, and we walked on.

We were getting close to our house and Appan was walking happily without saying a word. Just around the next turn, we would reach the spot where I knew my little catastrophe was on full display. I felt nervous and couldn't keep quiet any longer.

'Why are you not saying anything, Appa? I have managed to alleviate Mary Chechi. She has agreed that we can compensate her when we can do it comfortably.'

'Oh, come on. Are you saying that everything you told me happened for real?' Appan was still playful.

'Yes, it did. But like I said, I am not very sure how,' I insisted, and we took that last turn at that exact moment.

Appan was horrified.

'Oh my god! You hit the wall down?' Appan's cool vanished, and he ran straight to our car.

'My goodness, this looks really bad. You forgot to use the handbrake and now you're claiming the car moved on its own!' Appan's face was filled with indignation.

'Appa, do you think I am crazy? How would I not pull the handbrake up? We've had the car for four years. Has anything like this happened before?' I protested, raising my voice, not forgetting to sound emotional.

Appan calmed down a bit.

'Okay, never mind. Let's be thankful that nobody was hurt. Just imagine if someone had been on the road. Anyway, don't tell anyone about this; it would be embarrassing. And you, there's no need for you to feel bad. After all, it's not like you intentionally drove and hit the wall. We'll take the car to the service station tomorrow morning and have them inspect it. Our insurance company will cover most expenses, so everything will be fine.'

I felt relieved. Typically, Appan would have set me ablaze with his reprimands. Maybe it was a day with luck on my side; he closed the chapter with a pat on my shoulder and a smile.

Later that night, I felt genuinely emotional as I thought about Appan. He was so kind-hearted and understanding. He could see that I was upset about not getting the job, so he didn't say anything harsh as he didn't want to make me feel even worse. It took me a while to fall asleep that night.

I woke up in the morning to the unusual sound of chatter in our usually peaceful home compound. People were talking, and I could hear someone opening and closing our car door several times. I cautiously stepped out of my room, tiptoed to the front door and peeked outside to see what was happening. I saw a small crowd in the front yard and a few more people across the road examining the collapsed wall. Both groups seemed preoccupied with whatever they were discussing.

One of our neighbours, Shaju Chettan, had opened and closed the car door. He seemed focused on something, thoroughly engrossed—God knows what. As I rubbed my eyes to clear them, the faces swam into clarity: Thomas Chettan, Josettan, Puthenangadi Francisettan and Appan's walking guild member, Varghese Maash. But when I saw the man leading the crowd enthusiastically recounting yesterday's incident, my heart sank. It was Appan!

'He didn't activate the handbrake, that's for sure. He had returned from college feeling tense about some other things. It happens; these youngsters can be so careless, as we all know. It's not a big issue, though, as we had insured the vehicle,' he said, clearly enjoying every moment of the storytelling.

I couldn't believe it. How! Just the night before, the man had left me feeling emotional with his line, 'You don't worry. And don't tell this to anyone. It would be embarrassing.' Here was the same man who was just killing it with his speech before everyone.

I shut the door, making sure I made no sound. Gauging the impending shame and the challenge of facing the people in the vicinity, I felt my head spin. That was when the worst happened. I heard Appan summoning me from outside.

'Joseph, have you woken up yet? Come and take the car out. We have some things to do. Annamkutty, go wake him up,' he instructed aloud, expecting Amma or me to respond. In the exact moment I considered running back to my bed to pretend to be sound asleep, Amma caught sight of me.

'Here, have some tea, and go take the car out,' she said, extending a steaming cup towards me.

'How am I supposed to go out now, Amma? Won't I have to answer all their questions? It will be downright humiliating! Appan is a cheat. He let the whole town know!'

'Eda, to claim the insurance money, we need a photograph of the car at the accident scene. That's why he asked you to take the car outside and click such a photograph. Don't waste time. Finish your tea and go take the car out. Place it as close to the wall as it was yesterday and take a picture.'

While brushing my teeth, I looked at myself in the mirror. 'Poor little fool, oh yeah, I was a fool, uh oh. Oh oh, poor little fool, I was a fool, oh yeah.' The old song spun around my mind, sounding like some bizarre nursery rhyme.

I felt ashamed of myself. I finished my tea, grabbed the car keys and opened the door. The first person in front of me was Francis Chettan, and he didn't have to prepare for even a second to give his remark.

'You are brilliant, Joseph! Otherwise, how would you have managed to do this? When you switch the vehicle off, the first thing you must do is pull the handbrake up. You should ensure that before you step out.'

Next came Varghese Maash.

'Actually, how did it happen? Why did the car take time to roll out even after you did not activate the handbrake? How did it muster the might to open the locked gate?'

All that I felt was fury. Antagonism!

I wanted to say, 'It must have been divine intervention. Let the ones who understood the truth praise the Lord. Glory!' And I would have, but I stopped myself, considering that Varghese Maash had been my teacher at primary school.

I started the car and parked it next to the crumbled wall, reconstructing the crime scene exactly as it was the day before. Looking out of the driver's window, I called out to Appan, 'Appa, take a picture.'

'Eda, you click one yourself; it won't come out right if I do.' he responded aloud with equal zeal, without giving the slightest consideration to what I had said.

'It would have been easier to kill myself,' I mumbled inaudibly as I got out of the car. I suspected that the crowd had grown in size; yes, it actually had.

'Hey, what's going on?' asked every passer-by. To cut a long story short, I was humiliated at an elite level.

Watching Appan's innocent behaviour and naive gesticulation, my mind told me, 'There is no way he could be intentionally insulting you. Maybe he is just sharing his confusion with others so that he can figure out how the car may have driven itself into the crash.'

The repair expenses exceeded the insurance coverage by Rs 7,000. However, the embarrassment faded quicker than expected, and the fender bender did not cause the projected psychological and sociological harm.

Weeks passed peacefully and then came a Sunday. After attending the Holy Mass, I strolled to the cemetery to visit my deceased kinfolk. On the way, I encountered Franklin, the son of my Class Eight English teacher, Francis Maash.

'Joseph Etta, you demolished your neighbour's wall. Was feeling bored, yeah?' He giggled at his own wit.

'Excuse me?' I asked, solemn in my tone.

'Your Appan told that story in our class yesterday! Oh, God, we all laughed till our guts hurt!'

With an indifferent expression, I told him that I had always enjoyed demolishing walls with whatever vehicles were available. With an equally indifferent strut, I went on to say hello to my old folks in the cemetery. I started walking back home. All the way through, I framed questions to ask my father. When I finally opened our house's front door and entered, I saw my father reclining in his easy chair, merrily going through the day's newspaper.

'Appa, so you are going around spreading my wall incident all over the place, right?' I got straight to the point. 'Weren't you the one who magnanimously suggested that no one should know about it if we don't need any embarrassment?' I couldn't conceal my annoyance.

His eyes widened in excitement as he folded the newspaper.

'Wow, so people have started asking? That's great, and it's exactly what we need! From now on, you'll never forget to pull the handbrake when you leave the car. What would have been the best outcome if I had scolded you that day? Maybe you would have said something unreasonable in trying to defend yourself. Also, there would have been a chance that you might repeat the same mistake someday. But now, with someone or the other asking you about it regularly, you won't ever forget.'

'Oh, so this was a well-planned scheme like in vendetta movies.'

'Yes, but with noble intentions.'

'Still, in the last four years, did I ever forget the handbrake? Have I ever made a single scratch on the car? Did you have to humiliate me all over the town for the first slip-up?'

'Eda, we eat good food every single day of our life. But does that mean we won't die if we eat poison just once?'

'That analogy doesn't suit this situation,' I objected.

'It need not.'

'Okay, let it be. Just remember, Appa, you are nowhere close to perfect. I will also get opportunities like this. But rest assured, I won't act this cheap!' I declared.

'That is up to you. Listen, the estimated cost to rebuild that wall is around ten thousand. As you know, the wall has no insurance coverage.'

'You keep an account of it all. I shall repay you when I get a job.'

This incident brought about a significant change in my life. I pulled up the handbrake every time before getting out of the car—it became as ingrained in me as washing my hands after every meal. As I write this today, four years have passed since I got a job and reimbursed Appan as promised. But you know what the problem is? I took down only a small part of that lengthy wall. The reconstructed section, which I funded, still sticks out like a big white button on a black shirt. Even now, some unsuspecting passers-by ask, 'The wall looks odd. Who did that?' The next second, I startle them by turning into Robert De Niro from Martin Scorsese's *Taxi Driver* and ask, 'You talking to me?'

THE LOVE THAT WENT UNLOVED

'In the end, only three things matter: How much you loved,
how gently you lived, and how gracefully you let go
of things not meant for you.'

—GAUTAMA BUDDHA

Do you remember that time you borrowed a pen from your friend in class when you ran out of ink? There's a friend of mine whose heart I have always wished I could borrow for a while. Not to use, but to give it all the love it deserves. His name is Albin. We are friends: Nibin, Nirmal, Albin, his wife Rose, Rose's sister Ann, and I. Albin's love for his wife always astonishes me; I have seen how much he cares for her. I have observed how he treats his wife's sister like his own sibling, offering her guidance and assistance. Albin always remembers to pick up a thoughtful gift—whether for anyone's birthday or a special occasion. It's never something generic. Instead, each gift is carefully chosen, a testimony to the thought and effort he's put into it. Whenever our group gets together, Albin always volunteers to cook. Everything he makes is delicious. They say that the love in the heart of the person cooking adds great flavour to the dish. I have often felt envious and wondered if I could ever love as deeply as he does.

'Love that goes unloved.' I first heard the phrase when Father Bobby Jose Kattikkadu used it while discussing St Francis in the programme *Gurucharanam*. This is the same saint we talked about in the Malayalam movie *Pranchiyettan & the Saint*. I always liked St Francis, but once I read Nikos Kazantzakis's book *Saint Francis*, I fell in love with that young man. St Francis talked and acted only out of love. Everything he did had a mischievous touch to it, and a hint of madness. He would kiss lepers' wounds, call the sun and moon his brother and sister, and much more. As he awaited death, he said, 'It's time for my sister Death to come.' He would ask his followers to dance and welcome death with love. Lo! Each of them had eccentricities that stemmed from love. Saddened by the sight of people not realizing that nature and every creature around are signs of God's love, he cries out loud on the streets, 'Love, oh, my dear, love going unloved!'

The ability to deeply love someone feels like a blessing. Even the pain of love carries with it the scent of love. I keep telling my friends that being unable to love anyone, even when so many love you, makes you feel sick of yourself. Having the innate ability to love someone is truly a remarkable gift. The burden of guilt carried by someone 'trying' to love is immense. They feel guilty that love doesn't come naturally to them, not blossoming from within. The most significant offense you can commit against someone who loves you is not acknowledging their love and turning a blind eye to it. Yes, to let love go unloved.

I want to talk about two loves that I ignored and, most of all, two individuals. Salvin Kannamballi is a friend of mine; in fact, he is almost like a brother. He treats me like a younger sibling and never forgets to send me birthday cards. I met Salvin on my first day at the seminary, where I had gone to train in priesthood after completing my Class Ten exams. Feeling homesick after leaving my family behind, I found solace in Salvin's friendship. Among the new students, I was the only one wearing denim trousers and a T-shirt, leading some to form a negative impression of me.

In the seminary, there used to be an activity called 'walk and talk' every day after meals. It was a rare opportunity to engage in open conversation with someone at the seminary, which otherwise emphasized on silence. In the early days after their admission, junior boys would take a walk with their seniors. In this walk, they were meant to share their sorrows, clarify whether the chosen path was correct for them and resolve any doubts. On my first day, Salvin, a super senior, accompanied me on that walk. Their agenda was to 'tame' me a bit. I cannot recall the specifics of our conversation that day, but I remember it was warm.

Months later, after we had become great friends, Salvin revealed to me, 'On the day you came here, I was sent to walk with you so that I could scare you a bit.' Like I said, he always looked at me like I was his younger brother. It was with him that I would share my questions, doubts and anxieties. Salvin used to write well. I remember him once allowing me to read his diary. But back then, I did not realize that he loved me enough to be okay with exposing his life in front of me.

He once told me about his village, the river near his house and how they would travel by boat. I told him I loved boat rides and mentioned that I remembered going on a boat with Appachan as a kid. That year, while we were all on vacation at our respective homes, I received a call on my home's landline.

'Joseph, I have arranged a boat. Come over; we will make your wish come true today!'

It was Salvin on the other end. I was watching some old movie on TV. I didn't want to go—not because I would miss the rest of the film, but for some reason, I just felt too lazy to go. Looking back, I realize that love and laziness never go hand in hand. I didn't love that man enough; it was as simple as that.

'I am kind of held up, Salvin. Maybe another time,' I said.

'Eda, I managed to arrange this exclusively for you today. We can spend a good amount of time on the boat and you can even have a go at rowing. It will be fun! Come quickly,' Salvin pleaded desperately.

'No, Salvin. I'm not really in the mood for all that. Maybe another time.'

As I write this today, I realize how cruel my words were.

'Okay, think it over and come if you can,' Salvin said before ending the call. He didn't show his disappointment.

I did not go.

What I did was rude, and I felt bothered by the imminent embarrassment I would experience when I met him next. I switched off the TV, went to my room and sat there for some time. Why didn't I go? Instead of idling the rest of the day at home, I could have quickly taken a shower, changed into fresh clothes and made the hour-long journey to Salvin's village. So why didn't I make that effort? The answer was simple: I never considered Salvin as important in my life as he considered me in his. Furthermore, I knew that even if I didn't go, it wouldn't diminish Salvin's affection for me and he wouldn't be upset with me. In relationships, there's a concept called 'taking someone for granted', right? It's the callous certainty that I won't be forsaken even if I forsake them.

I felt guilty when we met after a long time, but his face showed nothing but love and held nothing but a bright smile. We had spent only one year together at the seminary and kept in touch through occasional letters. Once, when a letter I sent to Salvin was late reaching him, he went to the post office to complain about it. This incident showed me how much my words meant to him. After realizing that being a priest wasn't my calling, I walked down the steps of the seminary for one last time. Salvin continued down that path, and our bond was kept alive by the birthday cards he sent me every year without fail.

Seven years later, he received priestly ordination. I participated in the first Holy Mass he led. When I saw him, wearing the priest's vestments, at the altar that day, my mind skied back to the snowy memories of our days together in the seminary. I stood there feeling lost, mulling deeply over the greatness of his heart, which could go on loving without complaining.

People formed a long line after the ceremony to kiss the new priest's hands. When it was finally my turn, tears welled in my eyes as I bowed, pressed my face against his hands and kissed them. Afterwards, I discreetly made my way to a corner of the church hall and watched as others took their turn.

Even now, I receive a card or a call from Salvin on my birthday. As for me? I don't even remember his date of birth. Even if it does strike me one year, I will surely forget it the following year. I adore him, as a younger brother does an older sibling, but, even today, I feel guilty for being unable to express it. Even though I am sure I am loved, if I cannot reciprocate that love, could the reason be selfishness? Nothing seems to happen naturally; I am still trying to love, making efforts at it and failing miserably. Now, I go on living, writing about love.

A distance, created entirely by me, stands between us today. The calls and the cards have dwindled. But still, there is one thing I can say without a speck of doubt. If I am in trouble, among the first five hands that reach out to help me, one will be Salvin's. The love of a brother from another mother, the love that will never forsake you even if you forsake it. Does Salvin love me like he used to? Does he still consider me his younger brother? Would he be reading this? Salvin, I anticipate a reply in the next birthday card you send.

As we move forward, I want to talk about my oldest brother, Adarsh. My birth had a negative impact on him. He is the firstborn and there is a ten-year age gap between us. At ten, he felt embarrassed to have an infant brother. It made him mad at me right from the moment I arrived on the planet!

When I was four, Adarsh took me to a salon in our neighbourhood for a haircut.

'Aren't you Jose sir's son? Jose sir has two boys, right?' Shivan, the salon owner, asked my brother.

'Yes, two boys.'

'Then who is this kid you have brought along?'

'This is our neighbour Rosily Chechi's son.'

Out of the awareness that Rosily Chechi's son was my friend Bestin, and that what my brother had just said was a bloody lie, I stared at him as hard as I could. When I sensed menace in the look he returned, I retreated and sat with my head bent low. That evening, I informed my parents about the incident. They questioned him, demanded an apology and had him kneel as chastisement.

Chettan's favourite pastime was scaring me. As a child, I was terrified of pressure cooker whistles. Whenever Appan and Amma left me in his care, he would fill the pressure cooker with water and make it whistle to frighten me. Tickle torture would follow the whistle torture. He would lock my legs between his knees, hold both my little hands down and tickle me. When I was almost about to die, he would spare me for a few moments to catch my breath and then tickle me again. At night, he would horrify me with ghost stories. In short, he found great pleasure in tormenting me.

When I grew up a little more, he went to Shoranur to pursue his studies and then started his first job. We didn't stay together for very long. My fond memories of my Chettan include that haircut, the endless tickles and pressure cooker whistles. But I must admit that these memories have only recently become fond.

When he received his first pay cheque, he bought me a toy bike that would spin with a key and two T-shirts that never fit me.

'In my mind, he was still tiny. I didn't know he had grown up,' was his explanation to Amma.

He was not at home when I decided to join the seminary after completing my Class Ten exams. I telephoned him and delivered the news. That was all there was to it. His marriage happened when I was in the seminary. I took special permission to be able to attend it. When his first child was born, they brought the baby to the seminary for me to see.

In essence, Chettan and I never shared any deep love or friendship. By the time I left the seminary, Chettan and his family had already moved to Dubai and had settled there.

Like the stereotypical Dubai man, he brought me perfumes, watches and chocolates every visit. He is a man full of love but doesn't know how to express it well. When Arun and I sent elaborate wishes on our parents' birthdays, Chettan would limit it to a crisp text: 'Happy birthday, Appan.' That would be it. Whenever my parents and I went on a long trip, the first call would always be from Chettan. He would ask, 'What's up? Where have you reached? Please pass the phone over to Appan.' That would be the extent of our interaction. He doesn't speak much.

I always felt that my Chettan is a good husband and a fantastic father. He's not too strict, and enjoys playing and laughing with his children like he's one of them. 'Saina Chechi is the one who takes care of the kids. She's a sweetheart,' I remember him telling me about his wife, Saina Chechi, when we drove together. As I express these thoughts, a hint of guilt tugs at me. You may be wondering why. I shall explain.

My first book, *Buried Thoughts*, had twenty-five chapters in total. The book was a reflection of my life up to that point. Two chapters focused on my brother Arun, while most mentioned our Appan and Amma. Not a single story was about my eldest brother, Adarsh. Even people I had recently met asked if the book included anything about them. A few of them seemed upset, saying things like, 'Oh, now I understand that I wasn't critical in your life,' when they couldn't find anything about themselves in my book.

My Chettan never complained. If you check his Facebook posts, you'll notice that most of the posts he has shared are my write-ups or something about my book. Today, many people are searching for and reading the book after I rose to fame as 'Joseph Annamkutty Jose'. Many ask, 'Why don't you write about your eldest brother?' What prompts me to write about him now is not the need to appear 'correct'. Rather, it weighs on my conscience that Chettan never even bothered to inquire.

I'm sure he must have felt hurt when he was disregarded in the book. So, why didn't he try to even the score by hurting me back? Why didn't he make even a casual complaint? Maybe his heart was big enough to understand me, or perhaps he thought, 'What's the point?'

When my brother shared an article about me published in the *Deccan Chronicle* on his Facebook page, I remember the caption he wrote: 'My brother.' Chettan's love for me and his pride in me were evident in those two words. Now and then, when he critiqued some of my writing on Facebook, he always used the gentlest of words. He spoke to me when I became fed up with my first job and decided to resign. He said, 'Don't rush into a decision; take a trip, clear your mind, and then decide.' His words were few, but they filled me with immense confidence because of the calmness in them.

Some time ago, when he returned from Dubai, we sat on his terrace at night, chatting and enjoying a drink in the cool drizzle.

I remember him asking, 'I have been following your write-ups, and they are improving. Do you watch movies by Padmarajan?'

He continued, 'Try watching the man's films: *Arappatta Kettiya Gramathil*, *Innale*, *Season* and *Thoovanathumbikal*. They are capable of giving your thoughts a new sense of direction. Throughout my life, I have truly admired only three individuals: Padmarajan, Sachin Tendulkar and A.R. Rahman—each is an inimitable talent.'

That evening, he inquired about the progress of my book sales and other routine nitty-gritties, but he never asked the one question I so wished he had asked: 'Why did you not include even a line about me in anything you wrote?'

That never came.

Whenever I have questions that I feel would end disastrously if asked directly, I resort to writing. Sometimes, it's a social media post; other times, it's a chapter in a book. I'm sure that once he reads this, Chettan will give me a call. I wonder what he will have to say.

I carry a heavy book of debts—debts of love I failed to return. Everything I write here is a remembrance of the love of certain people. Those who loved me did so without complaints. Or can love only be called love when there are no complaints?

Love becomes complete only when you start to love the other person's shortcomings as well. The only true love is the one that liberates a person from unnecessary shame, regret and certain wounds. You know that you love somebody, and you are happy about that. You know it can go unrequited and you know it may not last. Still, you can love; that is what makes the word 'love' magical. Love doesn't snatch anyone from anyone nor does it seek to possess anyone. Love loves! Unselfishly, at times, forgivingly, and, at other times, with teary eyes.

God, teach me to love a little more than I am loved.

I dedicate this one to my eldest brother, Adarsh.

GURU

'What the teacher is, is more important than what he teaches.'

—KARL A. MENNINGER, American psychiatrist

The church was celebrating a festival and a grand procession was moving forward. In this neighbourhood, there was a man named Martin, who had the reputation for being a hooligan. He would do things as he pleased, regardless of whether onlookers found it appropriate or not. On that particular day, he stood along the parade route with a giant balloon hidden under his T-shirt and a sign hanging from his neck, which read, 'Who got me pregnant?' At that moment, something amusing happened. Thomas Master, who had taught Martin in primary school, walked by, and Martin noticed him. Martin, 'the hooligan', instantly burst the balloon and relieved himself of his 'pregnancy'. He hurriedly flung away the board hanging around his neck, smiled and, like a schoolboy, stood in respect of his old school teacher.

This visual from my childhood remains intact in my memories. It never seems to be of any importance whether they still teach or not, teachers remain teachers, no matter what! I once hired an auto-rickshaw and the driver asked me where I wanted to go. I replied, 'Please drop me at the house of Jose Master, the teacher who used to teach at Star Jesus School.' The auto driver, who was in his forties, smiled radiantly as he said, 'Jose Master taught me English at school!'

When I got home, it was late and I was exhausted. I had planned to take a shower and go straight to bed. I went to my room, locked the door and entered the bathroom. After a minute, Amma knocked on my door and called for me. Despite bellowing several times that I was already in the shower, she kept knocking. Exasperated, I turned off the water, wrapped a towel around myself and opened the door.

'What is it, Amma?' I asked, wiping water off my face.

'Eda, Elsy Teacher called. She talked a lot about you and said she had something important to tell you. You should call her back; even if you do it tomorrow, it's okay. Here, keep her contact number right away,' said Amma, extending the paper with Elsy Teacher's number on it. I asked her to keep it under the soccer ball paperweight on my writing desk.

Elsy Teacher. She was my favourite teacher, my class teacher in Class Four. I wondered why she had called me. I found myself reflecting on our times together.

Amma and I visited the teacher's house three years ago for a funeral. I vividly recall standing there, observing Amma comforting Elsy Teacher, who was utterly drained from grieving. 'What will I do, Annamkutty teacher? Who do I have now?' Elsy Teacher cried, holding Amma's hand tight. They were once teachers at the same school. Elsy Teacher's husband had died in a bike accident while on his way home from work. At times, God displays cruel humour—ordinary people may not be able to interpret it as part of the divine plan or any esoteric scheme.

Some deaths leave only after extinguishing the will to live in those who remain. I couldn't find the courage to look at Elsy Teacher's face that day. I chose to leave the house and wait. After some time, Amma also came out, tears streaming down her cheeks. I still remember what Amma told me that day during our drive home.

'Paul meant everything to Elsy—he was a wonderful husband and a great father to her children. He took care of even the smallest things in their lives, whether it was in the kitchen, managing finances or looking after their children's needs. He lived for his family and prioritized them above everything else. While his colleagues and friends were busy with social work or church activities, the family was everything to him. How will Elsy cope with this loss?'

My lower primary school was close to the school where my Amma taught. When I was in Class One, as I walked back home with Amma, Elsy Teacher would accompany us halfway. Even back then, she was skinny, with a calm face which always held a shining smile. Sometimes, as we walked together, I would hear Elsy Teacher inquire about my elder brothers to Amma, as she had taught them as well.

'When Joseph reaches Class Four, I would have taught all three of your children,' Elsy Teacher would tell Amma.

'Both your brothers were wonderful students. You will also be, won't you?' I remember her asking me one day.

When I reached Class Four, Elsy Teacher was our class teacher. Back then, teachers whacking students was a common practice and was not considered an offense. But even in those times, Elsy Teacher never once hit us.

She was a teacher who gave instructions to her students most lovingly.

'Before our class tomorrow, all of you must study this, okay?'

'All of you should be good kids and don't make too much noise, alright?'

Such were her instructions, every one of them as sweet as it could possibly be.

If there was any student who took the freedom that she gave for granted, it would have to be me. I would make funny comments while she was teaching. She never reprimanded me but would stifle a laugh.

'Joseph, keep quiet!' would be her response at the most.

'Among your three boys, he is the most mischievous,' she once told my mother, tapping me affectionately on my cheek.

Elsy Teacher taught Moral Science when I was in Class Four. She was the only teacher who would take us out of the classroom and let us spread out in front of the big tamarind tree in our school compound. It was a treat exclusive to the Moral Science classes. The big old tamarind tree had the aura of a wrinkled yet graceful grandmother. Her canopy provided a soothing shade for countless generations of students. It's painful to think that the grandmother tree is no longer in the school premises. Like most good things, time has reclaimed it for eternity.

One day, Elsy Teacher was teaching us under the tamarind tree.

'Growing up as students who carried goodness' was the day's topic.

'People who have goodness in their hearts will be healthy, no matter how old they grow. So, if from now on you start living your life doing good for people around you, you will be able to jump and run around like this even when you are old. So, are you all ready to be good kids?' Elsy Teacher asked the class with a smile.

The question did not take even a second to wake up the cynic in me.

'Teacher, we are ready to do good and all that stuff. But what guarantee do we have that it will assure us of good health in our old age?' I stood up and asked.

She scowled at me, asked me to sit down and then started explaining sweetly.

'You all know Mother Teresa. The world calls her the mother of the poor. Her face is crumpled, her hair grey, but do you see how enthusiastic she is? Even at this age, she is running around doing her work. That is why I tell you, good-hearted people will live a long and healthy life.'

My reaction to her explanation both startled her and made her laugh.

'Dear teacher, I saw in the newspaper that Mother Teresa is hospitalized. They say it would be hardly one or two weeks before she takes her flight back to the heavens! Now, what say you?'

She couldn't help laughing at my comeback. I'm not sure what made her laugh: The earnestness of my question or the fact that it was coming from a little mouth. She asked all of us to stand up, asked me to stay back and told the other students to return to our classroom in a line.

'My dear Joseph, are you supposed to talk about such great people like that? It is very wrong. Never do such things again. I sent the rest of the students back to the class because I could not control my laughter. Never tell this kind of joke while I am teaching. Okay?'

When I returned home that day, my mother gave me a good dose of advice. Elsy Teacher had told Amma a few things, which Amma conveyed to me.

'Teacher, please tell him not to say things like that in class. Some things that he says surprise me and make me laugh at times. I usually pretend to ignore those and continue with the class, but he has started doing it more nowadays. Please tell him to be more attentive in class.'

On the last day of Class Four, when Elsy Teacher came to the class, she had two beautiful pens in her hand. They were special pens that none of us kids had ever seen before. Each pen had four refills of different colours inside. For the first time, we witnessed the wonder of a pen that could write in four different colours.

'I have two pens with me. I intend to give them to two of my favourite students.'

The first name that she called was a girl: Sangeetha S. Menon. She was my rival and we would constantly quarrel in class. In the class photo, she had drawn on my face with her sketch pen, making me look ugly. That's how much we disliked each other. However, she was a good student, had a beautiful singing voice and was skilled at storytelling.

I was sad and angry when Elsy Teacher called Sangeetha S. Menon's name. She could have gifted that pen to anybody, but why did it have to be Sangeetha S. Menon?

'Now, I will call out the name of my favourite among the boys. Joseph K. Jose!'

I was overjoyed for two reasons. First, I immediately wanted that pen the moment I saw it. Second, not receiving it would have left me humiliated in front of my greatest nemesis at the time, the tiny Sangeetha S. Menon. That day, as the class was ending, Elsy Teacher held me close and shared some words with me. Those words have stayed in my heart forever.

'Joseph, you are a chatterbox. You are very humorous. I was always happy to teach the class that you were part of. You think differently from other students. You are "creative", like they say in English. I will miss you. In the future, when you become a movie actor, writer or something like that, I hope you will remember teachers like me.'

When you read these lines today, you might think, 'Oh, he finally wrote a book and went on to act in a movie too.' I also thought that when I wrote that part.

In the past twenty years since, I must have crossed paths with Elsy Teacher at least ten times, at ten different places. Each time we met, I was in a different phase of my life. During every chance encounter, she introduced me exactly the same way to whoever was with her that day. She would say, 'Here, this one is my favourite students.'

Each time she said this, I felt a great responsibility. I was my teacher's favourite student and I felt a duty to never disappoint her. This feeling became deeply rooted in my mind.

After Class Four, I encountered many teachers in my life. Some of them disliked me, criticized me with harsh words and raised complaints about me. However, if there was one teacher who often encouraged me, it was Elsy Teacher. I am sure that I was not a stellar student; I made mistakes and had my flaws. However, her eyes always found a glimmer in me. Every time she met me, she made sure to nurture it so it would shine brighter and grow stronger.

Today, I am known for my 'talks'. Many people tell me, 'You speak beautifully.' But my Elsy Teacher was the first to say that, even when nobody else did.

I made a video on 5 September, which was Teacher's Day. In the video, I talked about my teacher, Elsy. I wasn't sure if she had seen it, so I planned to ask her about it when I called her the next day.

The following morning, I got Elsy Teacher's call on Amma's phone before I could return hers. Amma passed the phone to me, gesturing that I talk to her.

'Hello, teacher, it is me, Joseph,' I said.

'My dear son, in the last two years, there has not been a day when I have felt so happy. My daughter showed me the video where you spoke about me. To know that you still remember all that makes me happier than I can explain. Since the passing of my husband, I haven't laughed heartily even once. When you recounted all those incidents, recollecting them individually, son, I laughed from my heart.'

My old teacher's voice was trembling, making me feel emotional.

'Teacher, I did not say anything that wasn't true. There was never another teacher who adored me like you did. I was sharing my love through that video. I am glad to hear that it made you feel happy.'

'Son, I am retiring this year. I wish you could be present on the day. They are planning to give one, only one among all the kids I have ever taught, an opportunity to give a felicitation speech. My wish is that you do it. I am aware that you are very busy these days. But, if possible, you should come, Joseph.'

'Teacher, I would be delighted to do that. Just let me know when and where. I will be there!'

'I'm thrilled, my son. The fact that a student remembers a teacher even years later is the greatest recognition any teacher can ever get. I'll send you the programme's invitation card and give you another call as a reminder. And all the best for everything you do, son.'

Within a week, I received the invitation card from Elsy Teacher.

The programme was on 8 February at St. Thomas L.P. School, Edakunnu. When I looked at the schedule, I saw 'Felicitation: RJ Joseph Annamkutty Jose' printed there and I felt extremely happy. It felt very special to get the chance to honour the same teacher who, on the last day of Class Four, had gifted me a pen and a heartfelt wish that inspired me to move forward.

Elsy Teacher was retiring from the same school where my Amma had studied in her childhood.

When I cut the call, Amma said, 'I will also come with you. I would also love to meet Elsy Teacher once again.'

So, Amma and I went to be part of Elsy Teacher's farewell function.

When Elsy Teacher spotted us, she excitedly approached us and greeted us. She then took us inside, and served us tea and snacks. Her relatives were also present. Even that day, she introduced me the same way: 'Here, this one is my favourite students.'

In my life, I have delivered felicitation speeches at multiple places on multiple occasions. However, if I ever spoke straight from my heart, it would be that day. I will conclude this chapter by revisiting my words for Elsy teacher.

> Hello, everyone. My name is Joseph and I am an RJ. When you heard the term 'radio jockey', you might have already guessed it: A guy who goes on talking. During my days at school, I was a chatterbox. Many teachers complained about me, even declaring that teaching in a classroom where I was present was difficult.

But only one teacher always said, 'You are talkative and good-humoured, and I love teaching in a class that you are part of.' That teacher is sitting here today, in her yellow saree, smiling as she always does, our Elsy Teacher. She once told me I was creative and could become a writer or a movie actor someday and gifted me an imported pen. Today, when thousands of people listen to me on the radio and watch my videos on their mobile phones, dear Elsy Teacher, I have just one thing to say: The pen you gifted me that day had a significant role in this larger scheme of things.

A line that William Arthur Ward said about teachers comes to my mind: 'The good teacher explains. The superior teacher demonstrates. The great teacher inspires.'

One who inspires and influences students is the best of teachers. It is only because Elsy Teacher inspired a little fourth-standard kid that he is standing here today, capable of speaking like this from his heart. I present my Elsy Teacher to every student studying in this school as the most precious gift. If I cherish her even after eighteen years of her having taught me, it is not because I am a great student. It is just because she was always a great teacher. Let every teacher have students who forever keep their teacher deep in their hearts, like Elsy Teacher has Joseph. Thank you!

CAST AWAY

'Some people feel like they don't deserve love. They walk away quietly into empty spaces, trying to close the gaps of the past.'

—JON KRAKAUER, *INTO THE WILD*

It's the 2011 Cricket World Cup semi-final, and India and Pakistan are facing one another. Whenever the two teams play in a World Cup, it's dubbed 'The Mother of All Cricket Matches'. Sachin is at the crease with 23 runs. The young and talented bowler Saeed Ajmal hits Sachin on the pads and appeals for an LBW with great conviction. At first, it seems like Sachin is out, and most spectators groan. The umpire raises his index finger, declaring Sachin out, and the stadium falls silent in gloom. However, Sachin decides to review the decision. Each team only has three reviews against the umpire's decision. When the Hawk-Eye tracking is displayed on-screen, the stadium's enthusiasm soars as it becomes clear that the ball was just a hair's breadth away from the stump. The umpire changes his decision and Sachin continues to play. He makes a brilliant knock of 85 runs, setting the stage for India's victory in that match. In the final, India beats Sri Lanka and, after twenty-eight years, we lift the World Cup!

Reflecting on this, I wish we had a review system in our lives to help when anything seems lost, or win in situations where we feel defeated.

I got a call on the office landline; a youngster was at the other end.

'Chetta, I am calling from Pattambi. I would like to meet you in person. May I come to your office tomorrow?'

'Isn't that a pretty long travel? If it is something that you can speak about over the phone, we can discuss it now.'

'No, Chetta. I wish to discuss this in person. I shall come over tomorrow. Kindly keep some time aside for me.'

I sensed a certain helplessness in his voice, so I agreed to meet him. The next afternoon, around 2 p.m., he showed up.

His name was Akash. With a long, lean face and sunken eyes, he appeared to be around twenty-two years old. He seemed a bit fidgety. We sat facing each other across a table in the office conference room.

'Chetta, I have watched every video of yours. I never for once thought that you would agree to meet me. I find it hard to believe that this is happening.'

His eyes appeared to harbour hidden sorrows and they frequently glanced out of the room's glass pane.

'Are you tense about something? Why are you looking out now and again? Is that a friend who has come with you?'

He leaned a little forward and spoke to me with a tinge of secrecy.

'Chetta, he is one of my very close friends. But what I am about to share with you is something that even he doesn't know. I am a bit worried that he will overhear me from there.'

'Just keep your voice low. It won't go out,' I said with a gentle laugh.

He took a deep breath and leaned forward. He looked like he was getting ready to discuss something that mattered very much to him. With a slight quiver in his voice, he began.

'Chetta, I have a friend … No, I *had* a friend. That would be more correct. It was a girl, not a girlfriend or a lover, but a great friend. She doesn't even talk to me anymore. A few months ago, we had a small argument. Hot under the collar, I blurted out a few things and she stopped talking to me. Chetta, last week, when I watched a video of yours, a thing you said stuck with me. "Nothing is too lost to be retrieved. No one is too far to be reclaimed. Resolution may be one confession away, right across an apology." You were also saying it was from some book you read …'

Having managed to vent that much, a smile appeared on his face for the first time. He continued.

'The day I watched the video, I called her up. I asked her to forgive me and told her I wished we could be friends like before. She said nothing in response. She is still cross with me, Chetta. No matter how much I try to reason with her, she appears unmovable. I miss her friendship a lot. What do I do now?'

'How did your friendship start? Do you mind telling me in a nutshell so I can understand better?'

'Chetta, she lives near my house. There were issues in her family which eventually set her up for emotional and financial difficulties. I got involved in those troubles and our friendship started. I stood by her through everything. I even spent around twenty thousand rupees from my pocket to help her. Please don't take me wrong. I am not trying to say that she owes me or anything like that. I am just opening up because it is you. I have never had any romantic feelings or other inclinations towards her. It has always been fondness towards a good friend.'

The honesty of his words was evident on his face.

'We used to meet daily, just to chat. And we would occasionally go out too. Her friendship meant a lot to me. But gradually, her problems lessened and her life took a new direction as she went abroad for her studies. Over time, her calls became less frequent and she stopped checking in on me. She attributed our recent distance to her studies and busy schedule whenever I brought it up.

'We're all human, right? We're all sensitive enough to notice when someone is trying to avoid us. When she returned for the holidays, I couldn't hold back and ended up giving her an earful.'

'Akash, at times, words cut sharper than a sickle. Can you recollect what you told her?'

'I did not say anything abusive, Chetta. I asked her if I was just some toy to her, which she could throw away after use. I told all that to her face. I proclaimed we wouldn't meet anymore, turned around and walked away. But she never tried to call me back or asked me what made me say all that. Why didn't she ask me anything?'

I could feel the question hurting him inside as he spoke to me.

'Over time, a friend sent me the video I mentioned earlier. After watching it, I started feeling guilty. I wondered if I had been in the wrong. Were my words too harsh? Could they have hurt her deeply? These thoughts troubled me and I strongly wished to repair our friendship. This led me to approach her and apologize. How can I have her back as she used to be? And am I at fault?'

Beneath the black-framed, thick spectacles that he wore, I could see his sunken eyes moisten. Here was a young man who, inspired by my words, had attempted to win back an old friend, but had failed. What more could I tell him? As he sat in front of me, I could see the face of my long-forgotten friend Priya in his place and imagined myself as the friend he had just told me about.

Some people enter our lives like guest appearances in movies. Their screen time may be brief, but their presence can change the entire course of the story. The teary eyed boy sitting in front of me was like a guest character. He reminded me of Priya. Before I share with you what my response to that young boy was, I would like to introduce to you Priya, and the bond I shared with her.

I first met Priya in the chapel on the fifth floor of Christ College in Bangalore. I was starting college in an unfamiliar city under unfamiliar circumstances. 'I will pray and begin,' I thought while standing before the chapel. I took off my shoes and was about to enter when I saw her coming out. We noticed each other but didn't exchange a smile.

When we entered the classroom that day, we realized that we would study together for the next three years. The conversation started with us acknowledging we'd met at the chapel in the morning. During our discussion, we discovered that we both hailed from Venkatapura; I lived on 6th Street and she lived on 7th. I resided in an apartment with my brother, while Priya lived in a house with her family. After our classes that day, I asked Priya to help me find the correct bus to go home. She informed me that, unlike in Kerala, the buses wouldn't display the names of places on their boards but instead carried specific numbers denoting their routes. She also mentioned that all the buses numbered 340, 341 and 342 would pass through Venkatapura, and that we could travel together. I used to get off at the stop right before hers. We travelled together in the initial days, and one day, she suggested that I get off at her stop and even invited me to visit her home.

'Just come over, Jo. Appachan and Amma told me to bring you home because they wanted to meet you. You happen to be my only neighbour in our class, right?'

'Oh, why not? I will for sure get good stuff to eat, won't I?' I joked.

'You just come along, Chekka. I'll get you something,' she said with her characteristic chuckle.

We got off the bus and started walking. We strolled down a street with a distinctly labour-class air. Amma's words before I left home echoed in my mind.

'You should always keep one thing in mind: Your brother is spending a big sum for you to study in Bangalore at Christ College.

It is not like the colleges back here where middle-class students study. The students there are going to be very fancy and high profile.'

I remember thinking that this street, cutting through the slum, could be a shortcut to Priya's upscale residence. I strolled alongside her.

'This is our home, welcome,' she said, pointing to a very small house. I saw nothing close to what I had pictured; it was almost the opposite.

A very small house, its roof tiled. A contraption that made a not-so-successful attempt to look vaguely like a gate opened into the courtyard—the courtyard was so small it could barely qualify as a courtyard. Outside of the house, to one side, stood the family's only bathroom. A few garden plants stood on the compound wall and in the corners. How on earth did Priya reach Christ from here? Could it be that she was an excellent student and got a special seat? These were the thoughts running through my head.

Tea was served by Priya's mother—a sweet, talkative mother. We chit-chatted for some time. That was when I got to know that the crammed house wasn't even their own, it was rented. They asked me about my folks back home and all those usual things which are a part of an initial conversation aimed at getting to know each other better. They told me to feel free to give them a call if I ever needed anything. All the while, I could barely wrap my head around the fact Priya lived here. She had a younger sister; they were a family of four and the house looked too small to accommodate them.

Our friendship blossomed and I would visit their house from time to time. I had a lot of freedom with them; I could tell them things like, 'I'm craving beef curry tomorrow; I'll come over in the evening' and they would prepare it for me. I was treated like a part of their little family. During exams, I spent most of my time at her place. We studied together and she would set aside many household chores to help me with my subjects. I would always go to the exam centre from her house if any topic had even the slightest hint of mathematics. I would arrive at her home in the early morning hours and she would help me revise everything one last time. Then, I would return to my brother's apartment, shower, dress and return on my bike to pick her up, and we would go to the examination hall together.

In this time there was another girl in my life. I had intensely disliked her at first, but, over time, my feelings for her changed and I began to adore her. After the first semester, for the first time, I experienced what I thought was love. I'm not sure if it can be considered 'love' in every sense of the word, but I was strongly attracted to that girl.

'She is a very good friend of mine.' I resorted to that cliche that almost every boy in love depended on when it came to covering up their real feelings in front of other friends. Priya would constantly taunt me on the matter.

'Chekka, you are in love with her, right?' she would ask. I always laughed her off.

Before the start of our summer holidays after our first year, our class went on a trip to Wonderla. It was a fantastic day spent with my friends. Chettan's friend, Sally, had booked my ticket for Kerala. When I returned from the trip, I packed my bag and organized my things for my journey to Kerala. The following day, I was scheduled to take the Kallada Travels G4 bus to my native place in the evening. I wanted to say goodbye to Priya and Aunty before leaving, so I went to meet them.

'Jokkutta, it's been a while since I last saw you. Why don't we hear your trademark "Prepare chicken for tomorrow, I will be coming" instructions anymore? Have you two quarrelled or something?' Priya's mother asked me right off the bat when she saw me.

'There's nothing like that, Aunty. I always think of coming over but I keep getting held up by something or the other. Where is she?' I tried to conceal my embarrassment.

When she saw me, Priya asked, 'What made you think of coming this way?' Her tone was sarcastic and her face held a forced smile.

I wasn't spending as much time with her as I used to and I felt guilty about it. Whenever I saw her in class, I used to make joking remarks instead of engaging in meaningful conversations. It wasn't intentional, but it rolled out that way.

'Jo, tell me something. Who am I to you?' she asked, looking straight into my eyes.

'Why are you asking this? As if you don't know …'

'What do I know?'

'Priya, please stop playing. We are good friends, and you know this too.'

'Jo, we went on a trip for the first time as a batch. Did you, even once, talk to me? Did you join me on at least one ride? You were with her all the time. I don't expect you to show me the same amount of love you show her. But you can pay a little attention to old friends, can't you? I know it is weird to plead for friendship, but still, I couldn't help saying this.'

I knew her question wasn't unfair. But all I had with me were wrong answers and justifications. Offering her my protest in the form of silence, I left without saying anything in response.

The distance between us remained even after we returned from vacation. Our friendship shrunk into the lukewarm smiles we exchanged in class occasionally.

The next year, on my birthday, I woke up early to someone knocking on my door. When I opened it, I found Priya standing there with a birthday cake in her hands, accompanied by her Appachan. It was the first time I had received a surprise birthday cake. We went inside, cut the cake and happily shared it. Her affection and friendship never wavered. The only one who had changed was me. I let go of the distance I had intentionally created through silence. After acknowledging my guilt and apologizing, we returned to being like we were. Unfortunately, that didn't last long. Our friendship encountered an unexpected setback, something I never saw coming.

One evening, a day before an examination, I went to her place to study with her.

'Jo, I shall teach you in our classroom from now on. We shouldn't be studying here anymore. Appachan told me some things the other day and I felt really sad.' She said, turning the pages of a book, trying her best to look casual.

'What did Appachan say?'

'Nothing big. And you needn't worry; I shall teach you in our classroom.'

'Priya, please tell me what Appachan said.' I raised my voice at her for the first time.

'Appachan said that the people around will start gossiping. He said that the women in the neighbourhood are already saying filthy things about you visiting now and then.'

Waves of shock rolled through me; it felt excruciating.

'Appachan couldn't understand our friendship, could he? Are these things the neighbourhood says or is it what he has on his mind?' Every single one of my words had more intensity than I intended.

'Appachan would have told that in some odd state of mind. It will be alright with time. You need not take it this seriously.'

Despite her attempts to appease me, I was hurt. I told her that we would talk later and I walked out of their house at that moment, declaring that I would never return again. After that, we never spoke much, not even in class. I was gradually losing Priya, a friend who had always taken great care of even the most minor things in my life.

As the end of my three-year stint in Bangalore approached, I realized that it was time to bid farewell. On the last day, before I boarded the bus to my hometown, I felt compelled to visit Priya's house to express my gratitude to her, her mother and her sister. Despite feeling some reluctance, I decided to go and thank them for treating me like a part of their family for so long.

As I approached Priya's house, her mother's face lit up warmly and she immediately invited me inside.

'No, Aunty. I am in a bit of a hurry. I have got to leave fast. Is Priya not here?'

'She had told me that you would be leaving today. You would still be angry inside, right? When will I see you again? When will I get to serve you a cup of tea? Please come in,' she said, trying to bottle up her sadness.

By then, Priya saw me and came close to the gate.

'Priya, I came to say goodbye to you. I don't really know when we will meet again. I will most probably be doing my MBA in Kerala,' I said.

With tears in her eyes, she gave me a poignant look conveying both love and anger.

'You go wherever the hell you want to,' she said, crying. Wiping her eyes, she ran into her house and vanished. Not saying another word, I left that place.

That night, I boarded the bus to Kerala.

It's been eight years since that day. The last text I received from her was after she read my first book. In it, when I wrote about the people who influenced me with love, her name was nowhere to be found. Without her, I would hardly have passed my exams. Even though the book didn't mention her name even once, Priya would have expected it because it talked about many people she knew. Even after realizing she was entirely left out, she chose not to voice any complaints at all. As always, her heart was big enough to message me.

'I read your book, good one, Jo.' So read her text.

In the form of rare chats, our friendship still lies somewhere, faintly glimmering under the ashes of time and trials. I know that with some fresh air breathed in, it could burn brightly once again.

When the youngster, Akash, from Pattambi, came looking for me, his voice seemed to be Priya's. It reignited my friendship with her, blowing air into embers, rekindling a fire.

While Priya's face shone brightly in front of me, I pondered about what to say to Akash. I believed that a confession would benefit us both.

'Akash, first of all, I want to thank you. You might be wondering why. I can feel what you are feeling right now because what your friend did to you, I had once done to a friend of mine. For a long time, she must have suffered like you. Maybe she has many friends now; perhaps she will never miss me anymore. Neither did I miss her all these years. But now, as I sit here talking to you, I am reminded of my friend Priya. I feel guilt and I feel pain. Everything comes to my mind: The way I used to make fun of her, how she would help me learn, how I taught her to read Malayalam and the tears she had in her eyes when we last met, everything comes to my mind.

'The way you came to me, maybe she also went to someone, carrying the wounds of a lost friendship. I don't know what the right thing to tell you is. But there is one thing you can be sure of. Even if your friend had deliberately overlooked you, or if it was her circumstances, there will be a day when she will face the memories of your friendship—a day when she recollects all of it with a lot of love. Akash, love never goes waste. The love we received once, the innocence of it, our hearts will remember forever, even if our brains forget it. It will still be covered in dust in some corner of our soul, possibly waiting to be retrieved. You need not worry and you should not chase unreciprocated friendships. You remain who you are. One day, they will return to your friendship, in a time still to come.'

Akash left, expressing his gratitude.

I wanted to make a call to Priya then and there. But make a call and say what? I decided to write it all down.

Dear Priya,

I know that being born and raised in Bangalore, reading Malayalam would be difficult for you. Yet, I hope you can still manage with whatever little I taught you in college. I have decided not to call you until this book reaches you and you have taken the time to go through these lines. It was essential to me that this book reached you before you bought a copy. In this specific copy that you are holding, I have written 'With love, Joseph' and signed it. Nowadays, people come to me with pieces of paper for my autograph, and I sign them. However, I must tell you, out of all the autographs I have signed so far in my life, if one were signed with my heart, it would only be this one.

See you soon!

With love,
Joseph

FRIEND

'I would rather walk with a friend in the dark than alone in the light.'

—HELEN KELLER

In the Iranian movie *Children of Heaven*, a young boy enters a running race to win the third prize, a pair of shoes. He aims to win the shoes for his little sister, who doesn't have any footwear to wear to school. During practice runs, he consistently finishes ahead of everyone else. However, on race day, he intentionally does not run to come first; instead, he desperately tries to finish in the third place. He keeps looking back during the race and ultimately crosses the finish line, though he falls due to exhaustion. He asks the teacher who helps him up, 'I finished third, didn't I?' The teacher replies, 'No, son, you finished first.' The boy cries upon hearing this, feeling like a loser despite being the winner. When he returns home, his little sister eagerly approaches him with hope, but the boy stands before her, his head drooping. The story ends with a reflection that some people, like the young boy, run all their miles for someone else.

I have ample material to fill a whole book, but I will attempt to introduce this person to you in just a few pages. I am talking about a very close friend of mine. To me, he is what today's youngsters in Kerala refer to as 'Chunk Bro'. I anticipate becoming emotional and shedding more tears than the ink flowing from my pen, so I have decided to keep it light.

This is a friend who has been with me for fifteen long years—a real friend. Suppose I knock on his door at midnight with a bottle of poison in my hand and tell him that I have made up my mind to die. Instead of getting tense or worried, he would make some black tea for us and just talk to me. I am sure our conversation would open the door to a new life for me. But having said that, I am not taking the 'how our friendship flourished and flowered' route that some memoirs take.

Let us take this story instead to a small tea stall at Desom Junction near the Cochin International Airport. Near the modest tea stall, we sit across each other at a blue sun-faded plastic table, nursing cups of black tea. It's almost midnight and it has been two weeks since I resigned from my job. While leaving that desirable job with attractive pay and social status, I gave myself numerous reasons to support my decision. Over time, terms such as business targets, profit and loss analysis, customer mapping and sales reports had become detestable to me.

'So why on earth did you do an MBA?' Please don't ask me that question!

Back then, a big slice of the human race seemed to be doing an MBA, so I simply followed suit. Opting for Commerce in Class Twelve exams took me to BCom and, as a natural progression, BCom took me to an MBA; that is how it went. After that, I worked for four years, although I can't say I enjoyed it very much. Now and then, I considered putting down my papers. By the way, 'putting down one's papers' is an informal English slang for resigning from one's job. The phrase can be further shortened to simply 'put paper'. So, for all these years, whenever I wanted to 'put paper', I was stopped by the emotional blackmail from my Appan and Amma.

But every time I contemplated resignation, I would ring this friend up.

'Da, I am done. I am going to put papers,' I would declare.

'Da, please don't rush into any decisions. How about we try for one more month? Just try working with more involvement. You might get back on track … Who knows? Should you give up a job that pays you so well? Furthermore, any other job would likely have similar problems.' His answers were always along similar lines.

But then, when I called him up for the fifth time and announced that I would 'put paper', he reacted differently.

'Were you a paper boy or something in your past life, you idiot? Your life is becoming all about putting paper! Okay, enough. Go ahead and resign. We'll handle the rest as it comes. No reason to stay is a good reason to go. Now, you don't need to overthink or discuss this with anyone. We will figure it out on the go.'

Without wasting a second, I went straight to shoot an email to my boss, and I resigned! At first, it felt like a huge weight had been lifted off my chest. My parents were excited about spending the holidays with my brother in Australia, so telling them the news that I had resigned from my job was difficult.

For the first two nights, I was able to sleep peacefully. But then it began to get me. Sleepless nights ensued, accompanied by some of God's honest truths. Inside my head, one question raised its head, then another, followed by another and another … They wouldn't cease. Have you accepted that you won't receive monthly income in your account anymore? Do you understand that money will soon stop coming from the ATM when you swipe your card? Has it hit you that you'll need to be more cautious when purchasing things online, like books, headphones, or anything else, really? At upcoming family events, you'll have to admit that you are unemployed. Jobless!

You might ask yourself, what job can I take now? Will the new job provide the same security and status as my previous one?

With a heavy heart, I wondered why I hadn't considered these concerns before sending in my resignation.

By the end of the next week, I was almost becoming an insomniac. That's when I called him and asked if we could meet. And that's how we arrived here: At a tea stall in Desom Junction, sitting across this blue, sun-faded plastic table, nursing cups of black tea. We sat there, determined to fix my future.

'Josappe, I've known you for many years now. You used to pray often, maintain a close relationship with God, repent even for minor mistakes and seek one confessional after the other. However, as time went on, you began reading a lot and growing through your reading. This led to a change in your views. Ideas like work being the only form of prayer started to influence your perspective. Sins that you once confessed with teary eyes are now being overlooked as "natural" and "human". I don't know how much of what I am saying you will agree with or accept, but we must retrieve that old version of you. I am not trying to say that all the troubles and tensions you are going through are happening because you pray less. But there are things beyond what we can ever fathom. There is someone, somewhere, designing roads and deciding directions for us. You should always nurture your relationship with Him. You need to recover a few traits you lost in your journey. At least for a short period of time, keep your logic aside and start visiting the church once again. Confess like you used to. Consciously, walk away from your present way of life for some time.'

Despite being known for providing practical solutions, his suggestions that day didn't directly address the crisis I was facing. It was the first time he had suggested something that seemed so unrelated to the problem at hand. When it feels like even your shadow has abandoned you and you don't know where to turn, when courage has long left your port, God sails towards you to salvage your situation in his ship of possibilities. That day, God reached out to me through his words.

There are often moments when we let go of our pride and surrender to something greater, and that's when the true meaning of 'change' becomes evident to us. I started looking for my former self, making an effort to wake up earlier and attend church. I made time for daily prayer and meditation, which didn't eliminate my anxieties and fears, but it did give me renewed strength and confidence to face them.

Days passed, and another Sunday arrived. Little did I know that it would deliver far-reaching consequences. After returning home from Mass, I turned on the TV. Every channel was bustling with discussions, debates and analysis of an appalling incident involving a film actress. They were mainly focusing on the fact that it was a woman who was brutally assaulted. Almost every prominent voice seemed drawn in, adding to the whirlpool of opinions. Politicians, media personalities, social figures and well-known individuals engaged in extensive discussions. The focus was on the violation of female respect in Kerala and the rising incidences of atrocities towards women.

For the first time, a conversation on a channel sparked an emotional reaction in me, which I could perfectly describe with a song from the Malayalam movie *Premam.* The lyrics—'Kannu chuvakkanu, pallu kadikkanu, mushti churuttanu aake viyarkkanu'—means, 'My eyes are turning red, my teeth are starting to grind, my fists are tightening, and I am sweating all over!'

I went straight to my room, switched on my mobile camera and spoke about a few things on video. I pondered over many thoughts before uploading that seven-minute video titled 'I am the change'. I asked myself, 'Is this necessary? What change will uploading this video bring about? I only had 2,000 friends on Facebook and, apart from being the target of their taunts and mockery, what impact can this video have?'

Since I had begun treading the path of good, I had a picture of Jesus on my wall. I remember that when I uploaded that video, I had placed my left palm on that picture, on Jesus's heart. That day, I had no prayers within me. After all, what is there to pray for when uploading a video? My mind seemed as clear as a white sheet of paper. In that video, I introduced myself to the world for the first time as 'Joseph Annamkutty Jose'. Looking back, I feel that I could have never even dreamt a dream of what happened next. The response to my video was phenomenal. Within a week, my Facebook friends increased to 5,000; my DMs and chats were flooded with compliments. Every major player in Kerala's media landscape shared the video as news. The number of people following my profile exceeded 20,000 in a month.

Then, one day, I received a phone call.

'Hi, Joseph, I am Smitha Ved Vaidehi, programming head for Radio Mirchi Kerala. I saw your video; it was amazing. Your words display great flow and ease, and your thoughts radiate clarity. What are you doing these days?'

'Absolutely nothing,' I replied, tactfully replacing the Malayalam answer that came to my mind with its English equivalent with the sole intention of sounding better.

'Joseph, we are looking for an RJ to join our channel. Are you interested?'

Before replying, I glanced at Jesus's face once more. The bearded, long-haired youngster who seemed to know it all was in the framed photograph on my wall for some time now. His expression seemed to convey, 'Just say okay, my boy!' As I write this, I am on the brink of completing two years as a radio jockey.

Today, if I thank anyone or anything for the happiness I enjoy in my life and profession, it wouldn't be that video. Instead, it would be to him, my friend, who helped me regain myself when I was lost. My gratitude would be to the womb of his friendship, which allowed me to be born again! This friend of mine is someone who had lost his mother when he was young. The word 'mother' would always appear in his speeches, writings and conversations. It could be because he has known such pain that he transcends into a mother tree for us, providing shade, shelter and solace. He carries an eternally welcoming womb of love in his heart, where anyone who enters is reborn: Better, brighter, braver.

He is not like a typical friend. When someone approached him feeling devastated after a break-up, he simply said, 'Let's take a walk.' He walked alongside them, saying nothing. Finally, he spoke gently, 'Remember that you have loving parents and friends who cherish you. The wind loves you, as do these trees. You have God watching over you so you won't stumble along your path.'

I want to introduce you to a young priest who speaks from the heart. I'd love to introduce my friend to you all. His name is Francis. He is my confidant, who taught me that a great friendship is the most incredible of riches that one can possess.

In the Malayalam movie *Immanuel*, Mammootty portrays a new employee of a company who helps an old lady, played by Sukumari, in her desperate struggle to get an insurance claim amount. The heartfelt words spoken by the elderly lady to the man who helped her resonated deeply with the movie audience.

'God bestows money and gold upon many people, granting them grand professions. However, it is only to one in a million that He gives His heart. Do you know why? It is to carry out His decisions here. Son, you have the heart of God. May God protect you.'

Francis, you have the heart of God.

I remember reading something on the cover of the book *Koottu*: 'If God were to ask me how long I want to live in this world, this would be my reply: "God, I want to live a day less than him. Because what makes this inconsequential life of mine beautiful is knowing that he is alive in some corner of this planet."'

Thank you for the dignity of life you chose to toil for others. Thank you for the arms you spread like an open door.

I would love to finish this chapter as if concluding a Holy Mass, with the prayer that the whole world recites for the priest in you:

Lord, distance my friend from the temptations of this world and keep him holy. May your divine love protect him from the deviousness of the world. May his efforts reach fine fruition. For those who receive his service, may it bring them joy and relief here and beyond and be their crown of eternal prosperity. Amen.

WHILE IT LASTS

'It is said that your life flashes before your eyes just before you die. That is true; it's called Life.'

—TERRY PRATCHETT, *THE LAST CONTINENT*

The young man who passed away didn't receive any tears from anyone. He was a troublemaker and caused constant problems for his family and neighbourhood. Sometime later, a girl is seen crying by his grave. Her father stands beside her, letting her lean on him. A passer-by asks, 'Who was this person to you?' The father replies, 'The eyes through which my daughter sees the world today belonged to him.' The youngster had signed papers approving eye donation after his lifetime. In a way, the eyes shedding tears for him were his own.

—AN EXCERPT FROM *AVASANATHE CHUMBANAM* BY NIBIN KURISHINKAL

Paul Kalanithi's *When Breath Becomes Air* is a compelling book that I highly recommend everyone read. It is filled with veritable insights and honest narratives. The book follows a young and skilled neurosurgeon who extends the lives of patients facing death, only to confront his own mortality when he is diagnosed with stage four lung cancer.

There is a part in the book where he awaits his impending death and asks his doctor, who is also his friend, about how much time he has left.

'If I have only three months left, I will spend it all with my family. If I have a year, I will write a book. And if I have ten years more, I will commence serving my patients once again as Dr Paul Kalanithi. Death may come later than I expect it to, but definitely earlier than I wish it does,' he wrote in his book.

The saying 'Live every day like it is your last' might sound cool, but if today were indeed your last day, how would you spend it? Some people might end up doing nothing but sitting still, filled with regrets about the things they never did, just waiting for the end.

That's what I feel.

We often hear two common questions: 'How's life?' and 'What are your future plans?' We usually answer both without hesitation.

'Not bad. Going on.'

'One more year and I will switch jobs.'

'I need to renovate my house in the next three years.'

'I will be the company's regional manager in five years.'

I believe we are all caught up in our web of plans. How often do we truly live in the present moment? How much do we appreciate the beauty of today? Some days, when I come home, tired from work, my mother brings me a glass of mango juice. I jokingly tell her, 'Mom, this is what they call heaven,' before quickly savouring the sweetness in that glass.

I attended a funeral before heading to office today, which prompted me to write this chapter. The person who passed away was Francis Chettan, our neighbour. His wife, Ruby Chechi, and his close relatives addressed him as 'Sojan'. I have known Francis

Chettan since I was a child. He was one of the biggest men in our neighbourhood and his voice had a deep, hoarse quality. His sudden death was quite shocking to me; someone whom I had seen since my childhood was no longer around. As I looked through the crowd that had gathered to pay their respects to Francis Chettan, I noticed his ninety-five-year-old mother seated near his body. Tears were streaming down her heavily wrinkled face as she tapped on his lifeless cheek and cried out loud, 'Sojan, my son, wake up!'

It reminded me of something I have always heard my mother say in her prayers: 'Dear Mother Mary, please don't ever let me have the fate you had.' How terrifying that ocean of sadness must have been when the body of her thirty-three-year-old son was taken from the cross and laid in her lap. And now in front me, a mother, nearing the sunset of her life, sits with shivering cheeks, mourning the death of her son. Dear God, did you give her such a long life just so that she witnesses this too? Age, which is supposed to enable humans to look at things objectively, did not help the old mother endure her devastation. The image of her crying like a desolate child still affects my heart.

Jeevitham Enna Albhutham—which means 'The Miracle Called Life'—is a book that contains the life experiences of Dr V.P. Gangadharan. The book, edited by the young writer K.S. Aniyan, takes readers on a journey through the lives of people affected by the perpetually cruel disease named cancer. Anyone with a heart will find it impossible to read this without shedding a tear. The characters and life situations portrayed in the book remain vivid in the reader's mind, like a fresh wound, much after they've finished reading it. Some very humble individuals embraced death with remarkable grace, while some sophisticated ones quivered in the face of it. Some drowned in regret, hurrying to achieve one thing after another, and not truly living life, while some souls witnessed their sibling's passing. Self-evidently, everyone spoke about the marvel of life. Mortals looked at life with longing, eyes gleaming when grappling with diseases or sensing death in the offing.

We always carry death with us. When death, the paramount truth, stands towering over everything, planning to do anything at all takes enormous courage. Death can summon any of us at any moment, at will. Oblivious to this, people continue indulging their petty egos and letting go of valuable relationships due to shallow pride. Quarrels linger on for years, even when a genuine smile can resolve them.

The great writer Khaled Hosseini says something similar in his classic novel *And the Mountains Echoed*. 'In our old age, lying on a bed, we are most unlikely to think, "I shouldn't have behaved that well to him"; rather, the regret would be about how you could have been nicer to people.'

The most profound realizations happen when we come head-to-head with death. I recall a son who remained estranged from his father due to a property dispute, and he cried like a baby when death drew close in the cancer ward. 'I want to meet my father right now,' he wailed.

Should you wait so long to confess a few of your mistakes? Should you wait so long to forgive another's?

'Forgiveness is the greatest gift of charity in Islam. I forgive you on behalf of Salahuddin and his mother.'

When you search for the above line on Google, a video will pop up. Salahuddin's father drew Tray Alexander, one of his twenty-two-year-old son's murderers, close to himself, as if he were holding his son, and said the above words. Then he said, 'My anger is at the devil for making you do such a heinous deed.' When the father said those words, Tray Alexander, sentenced to thirty-one years of imprisonment, burst into tears. It is those who are possessed who inflict harm, cause hurt and bring distress to others. Forgiveness is indeed the only path to liberate those caught by a spell. The Bible has a line that says, 'When you forgive a man, it ignites the embers of repentance inside his head.' It is not easy, but not impossible either. A thought may probably arise, 'What if the person doesn't transform despite being forgiven?' That thought may be put in your head by the same element we discussed a moment ago: The devil.

While pushing our days ahead, aren't the sorrows we hold in us countless? Aren't our lives lying entwined with innumerable threads of grief? Everything saddens us: Someone not replying even after the blue tick has appeared on the chat screen, a colleague mocking us, not receiving a call that you expected at midnight on your birthday and whatnot. Even a harmless scratch on the mobile screen distresses us to no end.

'When luck is on your side, ride it,' my brother once said. I vividly recall the moment: I had achieved an unexpected success in an exam and we celebrated with chilled beer. The line reminds us to treasure and celebrate all those little fragments of happiness we stumble upon on our path while treading this planet alive. Impermanence is what paints this world. Pleasures and pains come to us at unexpected times, adding an element of disbelief to our experiences. When people you've known for ages suddenly disappear and those closest to you seem to vanish into thin air, remember the small things that brightened your days. Your dad's check-in calls, your mom's reminders to eat while the food is still warm, your partner's eagerness for a movie night, or your best friend's invitation for a bike trip—these seemingly insignificant moments are great blessings to be cherished, at least within your heart.

Small moments like these are what make life so wonderful. It's like the old story of the man killing time on the riverside at night by throwing stones into the flowing waters. Only when the moonlight grows stronger does he realize that the rocks he had so casually thrown away were actually diamonds. The things closest to us deserve our utmost attention: Our fathers, mothers, spouses, children and friends who always stand by us. In the story of our lives, they are perhaps the most precious diamonds. Remember, your boss won't be the one to bring you a glass of warm water when you're down with a fever.

In pursuing various goals, let's not forget to cherish the people around us as they won't be here forever, just like everything else. The most primal feeling of 'having someone' still drives individuals to continue living. What if tomorrow we cease to hear them, or they to listen to us; or we cease to exist?

'Who has time for all this sentimentality while struggling to make ends meet? And for whom are we toiling if not for these few close to us? Nobody works solely for themselves.' I can see some raised eyebrows with these very reasonable responses.

I will conclude with a remark from a friend of mine. My reaction to her confession of feelings beyond friendship weighed quite heavily on her. I suggested reducing our interactions to help her move on. At least, that was my reasoning. After maintaining the distance I had built between us for a while, she sent me a text that was four paragraphs long. I will summarize its essence.

'To my father, I am just a burdensome responsibility that needs to be disposed of through marriage. I can't remember my parents ever asking me what I wanted or what my wishes were. I don't remember the last time my parents touched or embraced me. For me, happiness comes from one or two precious friends. This distance is never going to help me, Joseph. Can you at least stand by me as my friend for as long as you can?'

Like Mother Teresa famously said, not many of us are hungry for bread, but many are starving for love. Pause before bragging about never letting your home run short of anything. Maybe the place is short of love, a shortage that only you can fill.

I, Joseph, have been loved a lot, and that is possibly the only reason I can write about love. If you close your eyes briefly and think, you will know how much you have been loved.

And whom should I thank? I don't know. I am including the English translation of one of the most philosophical songs ever featured in Malayalam movie music.

Whom should I thank?

The father who, on that day, became half the body for me to be incarnate on this earth?

Or the mother who became the other half of it?

Or that womb which carried me for another ten months to make me myself?

The lines of destiny are disappearing, and so are the thoughts caught in spider webs,

Oh, dreams that threw the dice in all twelve ways; I wish you peace many times!

SAINTLY SOFT PORN

'I think God, in creating man, somewhat overestimated his ability.'

—OSCAR WILDE

I once wrote a post on Facebook titled 'To beloved Judas'. It was structured like a letter expressing my love and compassion for Judas. Even after walking alongside Jesus for three years, Judas betrayed him for thirty silver coins. I pondered whose mistake it was that Judas remained so cruel, even after spending so much time with the son of God. I concluded the post by suggesting that perhaps more attention could have been paid to Judas, as he was the odd one out in the group. Shortly after posting, I received several objections and was asked to remove it. Out of respect for others, and because my father is a catechism teacher, I deleted the post immediately.

Scene 1: Kalamassery Social Church

I sat alone in that chapel for a special prayer at the Kalamassery Social Church. On the altar, there was a wooden carving of Jesus's face. I'd been looking at that face for some time, before I found myself laughing. 'What exactly do you mean by this, Jesus?' I pondered silently. I noticed that she was still online and waiting for my reply. As I gazed at my mobile screen, struggling to decide, I clicked on her new profile photo and she looked exceptionally stunning. Three messages with question marks appeared in her chat box.

Scene 2: Kancor Office, almost forty days ago (Yes, a not-so-dull flashback)

Upon entering the office and clocking in at 10 a.m., the office security guard, Johnson Chettan, asked me to wait for a moment.

'Joseph sir, there is a courier for you; it arrived yesterday evening. Here you go.' He handed it over to me.

At first glance, it looked like a book. I turned it over; as indicated on the envelope, it was a personal courier from someone. I opened it right away.

The Purpose Driven Life by Rick Warren.

On the first page, there was a line written: To dear brother Joseph, your sister in Jesus, Leah.

Leah and I had studied together in college but we had never spoken to one another. I vividly remember my friends praising her stylish appearance at a fashion show. A few days ago, she had commented, appreciating one of my blog posts. This led to our first conversation: 'Thank you for the kind words,' I said. Whenever she spoke, there was an unbelievable amount of purity and goodness in her words. I never expected our conversations to evolve into spiritual discussions—not even in my dreams. She mentioned a book to me some time ago, and I had forgotten about it, but she had remembered. I was pleased to find that she cared enough to send it to me, despite my forgetfulness. The book is meant to be completed in forty days, with one chapter to be read and contemplated on each day. It's a book that aims to show us the purpose of life. I had a feeling that this book might answer some of my questions.

Since my childhood, I had always believed that bodily cravings were sinful. In religious teachings and catechism classes, terms such as 'sins against the body', 'carnal obsession', 'faulty conditioning' and 'pleasure compulsions' were constantly mentioned as things to avoid, and this perception became ingrained in me. It's natural to be drawn to the forbidden. Many young girls and boys are still burdened with guilt because their acts of self-pleasure are labelled as 'deadly sins'. I think it's time to rebrand this as 'pointless guilt'.

Right from my childhood, my mind was a spiritual warzone—a ruthless war between rights and wrongs never ceased. In many confessions, I have admitted my detours. I have prayed and cried out aloud to God to help me stay close to Him. I have received different answers from the other side of the confessionals.

'It's okay, child. Your desire to stay close to God is enough for your sins to be forgiven.'

'Don't repeat this mistake. It's not a big sin; it's just human.'

'You don't need to feel so guilty about this, son.'

'In today's world, not many youngsters confess these things like you did. God loves you a lot.'

As age progresses, what fascinates a youngster the most is probing into his physicality. The advent of mobile phones, WhatsApp and dedicated groups for sharing porn videos felt like highways being constructed to lead in that direction. All this made the war in my head fiercer than it used to be, but I continued to wage it.

As I matured, my perspective shifted, leading me to realize that the acts I once deemed sinful were really not. I gained a broader point of view and started thinking that there was no need for so much internal conflict to suppress our natural human inclinations. I no longer felt guilty and had fewer reasons to confess.

So that day, walking into my office with that book, I remembered the old, innocent version of myself who used to cry during confession.

I thought about the years when I tried to stay close to God, praying with rosary beads every day of my childhood, thanking God before bed, keeping a Bible by my pillow and experiencing the joy in my heart. All of those memories came flooding back to me. That book felt like an invitation to revisit all the lost goodness.

Suddenly, a new notification appeared on WhatsApp.

Akhil had shared a video in our group named 'On the Rocks'.

It was a WhatsApp group with only men as its members—a dedicated platform to share only adult content, including nude photos and porn videos. I did not open the video; instead, I left the group instantly. Leaving the group was a spontaneous decision. The next day, during our tea break, I became the centre of attention, like a hunted prey.

'Here is the saint!'

'It is just a matter of time before you beg to be added back to the group.'

'Staying away from this won't transform you. Transformation should happen in your mind.'

Opinions were thrown at me, but I didn't react because my desire for change was so strong. That evening, I went to the church, meditated for some time, prayed with a rosary and vowed to take up the forty-day challenge.

I took some precautions. Some of my friends, both male and female, would, at times, steer the conversation towards inappropriate directions at times. I told them I would take a break from WhatsApp for a while. One was a girl I knew from college who worked in Australia and used to be my junior.

'Why are you taking a break, man? Is it some kind of an amendment?'

She was a good friend, an intelligent girl I could open up to. I told her about my forty-day endeavour.

'Would it be fine to stop talking "adult" stuff to you? You don't need a break because you're scared of me! But jokes apart, wouldn't it be kind of like running away? You must win it, looking it in the eye. I won't lead you astray. But you must stay on WhatsApp. Maybe I can even help you with this challenge,' she told me.

She made sense, so we started the challenge together. I read one chapter daily for the first three days and reflected on its content. At night, I would receive a text from her saying, 'And we've completed the third day! You didn't deviate, did you?' She continued to send me motivational texts in the days that followed.

On the tenth day, I faced the first significant temptation. It came as a text from a girl who had read my book *Buried Thoughts*: 'I really enjoyed reading your book, especially the chapter "The Temptation". Your bold writing about such topics stood out to me. After reading it, I felt physically and emotionally drawn to you as a woman. Do you have any plans to adapt it into a short film? If so, I'd love to play the woman's role from that chapter, but only if you do the lead role.'

In that chapter, I had disclosed one temptation of mine. Even my family was against me publishing it. I checked the girl's profile. She was from Bangalore and she was beautiful. The last post on her page was a review of my book. She had read between the lines and written beautifully about the things I had tried to imply in that chapter. The post also included a selfie of her holding my book.

I read her text once again and took a few moments before replying.

'Thanks for the message. It's the first time somebody has told me that "The Temptation" is their favourite chapter.'

Her reply came faster than I expected: 'You are sinfully honest! Let me know if you are coming to Bangalore. Let's explore each other in some private place.'

It was the first time I had heard something like that.

I could feel my mind slipping. A sincere invitation to pleasure was right at my fingertips! I could hear a tide of questions rising in my ears. 'Who is committing any sin here? Who defines a sin? I am not pushing anyone to do anything unwillingly, am I? I am not hurting anyone either. What will I achieve living these forty days like a saint?'

Another part of my brain chimed in: 'Joseph, you are right in what you are saying. However, you started this, didn't you? You've managed to go through ten days beautifully. Are you so weak that you can't hold out for just forty days? The girl will still be there. Why can't you let it go for the time being?'

The war was beginning. One half of my mind began to wrangle with the other.

Then, I surprised myself with the reply I sent her.

'Thanks for the compliment. By the way, I read your review. It was beautifully written. Best wishes, God bless you. Bye.' That was my text. But I must admit that sending it wasn't as easy as writing about it now. The happiness I experienced that day was unique; you could call it the happiness of having triumphed over myself. In the days ahead, my 'fasting' continued strong.

On the eighteenth day, my friend James sent me some lovely photographs of a girl who looked really pretty and decent. He asked me if he could help arrange a marriage proposal from the girl's family.

'I am not planning to get married now. By the way, why do you have a sudden enthusiasm to get me married?' I asked him.

'Before dismissing it, take a look at this. You'll love it,' he replied and sent me a video. It showed the same girl undressing in front of a camera. At the beginning, she can be heard pleading, 'Please don't show this to anybody else.' I immediately deleted the video. By then, my mind had gained enough strength not to fall face down before solid temptations.

I rang him up right there.

'Why are you doing this rubbish? Did I tell you that I am eager to watch such things? Don't send me anything of this sort ever again!'

'Why are you getting angry? If you don't like it, don't watch it; that's it! I didn't know you had turned into a saint! Get lost, you ******!' he hurled cuss words at me and cut the call.

The days marched on. My mind remained a battle zone: The good and the bad traded shots. Regardless of the occasional flinching, the good kept winning. Those days were filled with peace and happiness, and I think there's nothing quite like rediscovering aspects of yourself that you thought were lost forever. Everywhere I looked, everyone I spoke to, even in my dreams and in the early morning light, I felt a sense of something divine. It's hard to describe the happiness that filled my body and mind.

On the fortieth day, a Thursday, I went to the church early in the morning and prayed earnestly. It occurred to me that, like Jesus, who had fasted for forty days and nights in the desert, I had also given up certain things for the same length of time. This made me feel loved and perhaps a little proud.

That night, I received a wedding invitation from a girl on WhatsApp. We had been Facebook friends for a year but had never met in person. Our friendship began when she contacted me after reading my book and shared her feedback. She had a lot of love and admiration for me. She worked in Chennai, and many of her colleagues had also bought and read my book based on her recommendation.

'Please come to Chennai sometime. I've asked you many times already. You have so many fans here,' she would occasionally complain. While I do visit Chennai at times, I tend to forget to meet with her.

'Congratulations, happy for you,' I replied briefly and drifted off to sleep.

Soon after, my phone beeped, waking me up. I scolded myself for not putting it on silent and fumbled in the dark to find it under the sheets. I realized she had sent a long text along with the invitation card, which I hadn't seen earlier. It must have been delivered later. I read through the message.

'Dude, it's my wedding next week, and I'll be resigning and returning to my hometown. All my friends here really want to meet you at least once. How many more times do I need to ask? You've visited Chennai many times but haven't even let me know. It's not fair to ignore someone to this extent. We all plan to take you out with us. If you can, please come this Friday. But I don't want to plead as I always do. If possible, make it on Friday, Joseph.'

I've had the chance to meet many good people on Facebook and some have become good friends over time. This girl has always been very supportive of me. She made sure that everyone in her circle bought and read my book. I knew I would have to visit Chennai next month to renew my brother's flat's rental agreement. So I reckoned that if I moved that task to this Friday, I could meet her without making an additional trip to the city.

'I am coming to Chennai. How many days will the outing be? And where will I stay?'

'Happy about your decision, Joseph! And don't worry, accommodation won't be a problem. One of your biggest fans is here. You can stay at his place. I will talk to him.'

She rang me up the next day.

'Joseph, our trip has been cancelled. It seems that the authorities have restricted entry to our planned destination. But that's okay; we will pick another place and go. Call me when you board the bus, and I'll come and pick you up.'

Scene 3: Chennai

I arrived in Chennai around 7 a.m. and called her. Within ten minutes, she came on her bike. I could see her face turning red and she confessed that she couldn't believe she was finally meeting me in person.

'Joseph,' she told me, 'there has been a small mix-up. Your biggest fan has had unexpected guests—his cousin and family are visiting him, which means you won't be able to stay there. But don't worry, we'll sort it out. There is a hotel near my hostel; I will book you a room there.'

'I must say the scene looks wholly bizarre! First, the trip was cancelled. Now my accommodation has been taken by a cousin of my so-called biggest fan. Now you understand why I never accepted your invitation to come over, right?' I teased her.

We rode together on her two-wheeler. Along the way, she told me the location of her hostel and asked if I could book an OYO room nearby. I attempted to book the room, but due to some technical glitch, I could not. She suggested we try booking a room at the hotel she had mentioned earlier. When we arrived at the location, I realized that the hotel was in a pretty secluded spot. We headed to the reception, where I inquired with the drowsy receptionist about room availability. He then explained the available options to us.

Single Room AC/Non-AC

Double Room AC/Non-AC

Chennai was experiencing its hottest weather at the time. I requested an AC single room.

'Why don't you book a double room instead?' she suggested. 'The price difference is minimal.'

'I understand, but why book a double room for just one person? Plus, I'll be checking out in the evening. It seems excessive to get a double room just to freshen up, don't you think?'

'I shall also join you. Would the double room be more reasonable then?'

For the first few seconds, I couldn't comprehend much. Did I hear her wrong? Or did she actually say that? What did she mean by saying she would 'join me' in the room? Thoughts flurried through my mind.

In Tamil, she asked the receptionist to give us a double room. He asked both of us to provide our IDs.

'What are you really up to? Hello?' I asked, laughing.

'You just give your ID. I am just trying to get you a bed where you can stretch out and be comfortable. Nothing malicious is intended, Mr Writer.'

We walked to the room together; I could feel my body heating up. Upon entering the room, her presence and the silence around us had already turned me on.

'You go change and freshen up. It has been a long journey, right? I shall wait here,' she said.

I walked up to her and gazed at her face, trying to clear my mind from all the confusion.

'I don't know if it's just me, but I had no strange musings until I arrived. But now, my thoughts are haywire. What's on your mind right now?' I asked.

'When you ask me that, I don't know. But I swear on my mother, I didn't have anything else on my mind until we got here. But when I saw you in person, I got excited. I want to talk and maybe spend some time with you. It'll be chaotic once we get to my friend's place, and you're leaving tonight. I'm sure we'll never meet again. Go freshen up and come back; I'll wait for you here,' she said.

'Hmm, I don't just want to have a conversation. I feel a different kind of urge,' I said, sensing the intensity in her eyes.

'Dude, I'm human too. The thoughts I'm having are probably similar to the ones you have on your mind right now. You don't feel like killing me or anything, right? Let's go with our instincts. After all, we're not kids,' she said.

I entered the bathroom. The breeze coming in through the small ventilator above the window made me smoulder. As the cold water from the shower hit me, my eyes closed, but my desires seemed to intensify. Behind my closed eyes, every thought I had was about the past forty days, but their chastity didn't seem to bridle my unchaste appetite. I wondered, 'God, how weak have I become?' The virtuous half of my mind seemed to have vanished. Every force, corrupt and carnal, seemed to take over me. I could hear a faint voice of reason in my mind trying to warn me, but my intense, primal urges overpowered it.

'Who named it adultery? Who named it evil? You are human; your creator placed your emotions within you and you did not plot anything,' I told myself. 'You held out as much as a youngster could do, right? To say "Go away, Satan" to every temptation, you are not Jesus Christ himself.'

When I came out of the washroom, my virtue was dead and buried. Pulling her close, I delved deeper and deeper into an unprecedented bliss until finally emerging from abyssal ecstasy. In that air-conditioned room, I perspired into a numbness.

Her touch was like that of a caring friend, her fingers gently running through my hair as if consoling a crying child to sleep. I felt both an overwhelming fear and deep-rooted guilt. At that moment, all I wanted was to flee from that room.

'Is there a church nearby?' I asked her. My voice was weak.

'Yes, there is a church a street away. But I am unsure if there will be a Mass now.'

'I don't need to attend Mass.'

'Are you looking to confess?' she asked with a simper.

'No, I just want to meet him.'

'Him … Who?'

'Don't ask me much more. Drop me off at the church, please. It will be enough if you can pick me up when I call.'

She sensed the change in my tone. We got out of there.

In the church, an old man sat on the last bench. I walked straight past him, up to the statue of Christ with His arms outstretched and stood directly in front of it. I could feel rage filling me from head to toe, and it started coming out as questions.

'Was it you? Did you, without a speck of mercy, push a person back into sin when he was trying his best to walk towards you and be like you? Don't you tell me it wasn't you! You don't dare tell me it was a test or anything like that! You sent temptations my way, beyond what anyone could possibly resist. I hope you won't put it on me that

I should have withstood it. I will consider it a gift you gave me ... I have nothing more to say.'

I kept looking into His eyes for some time, feeling sad and disappointed. I started speaking again.

'Did no one ever tempt you physically? I have read about how effortlessly you navigated the temptations of power and wealth. I have noticed how you, like us humans, had felt hungry, angry or saddened. You were the son of man, and that is why I can't help but ask you, have you never felt lust towards anyone? The Bible covers everything about how you went through everything human, but this ... Was this bit deliberately skipped?'

Jesus's face looked as if He was silently hearing me out.

Then, the blaming slowly ceased. I closed my eyes and, for some time, looked inward. I felt bad, the way one would feel bad after having yelled at a dear friend, and then I found myself slowly relaxing.

'I understand, Jesus. Blaming it on you for turning water into wine at the feast of Cana, a lot of buggers drink to their fill! Had you mentioned anything about your physical temptations in the Bible, those fellows would have run all over the place, indulging in adultery. Whether it had happened or not, it's good that you didn't mention them, Christ.'

Hearing the footsteps of someone approaching from behind, I turned around.

It was the old man sitting on the last bench when I had walked in.

'How dare you shout inside the church?' He glowered at me.

Before I could respond, he slapped my face hard.

I sat up in shock and looked around; all I could see was darkness. I could hear the fan above me rumbling. In panic, I scrabbled about until I found my mobile phone. I checked the time; it was two in the morning. I opened WhatsApp—below four other chats, there was a goodnight text from her, and when I opened it, the only thing that preceded it was the marriage invitation card. Realizing that whatever happened until that second was a dream felt unbelievable.

The next morning, while driving to office, I got a call from her. I hadn't entirely shaken off the relics of my dream. I picked up the call and put it on speaker.

'Joseph, is it a good time to talk? Got two minutes?'

'Good morning, bride-to-be! I am free; what's up?'

'I was planning to call you yesterday itself. That is when you wished me that dull "goodnight". So, I thought I would wait till today.'

'Yesterday, I was dead tired. Tell me, what is the matter?'

'Dude, you should come for my marriage. All your fans here are always asking whether you will come.'

'I will try! We have been friends for almost a year now and the first time we will meet is on your wedding day. Fate has its strange ways!' I laughed.

'Don't say that. How many times have I invited you to Chennai? Your brother even has a flat here, but still, you never came. Listen, I will be here for a week more, at the most. I am leaving my job. My fiancé works abroad, so chances are that I will also catch a flight with him. You come down the coming weekend and we shall take you around our Chennai! I can also put on a show before my friends by bringing you here.'

'I will try; I am not promising anything, though. I shall let you know by this evening.'

I cut the call.

Scene 1: Kalamassery Social Church

I sat there, gazing at the three question marks she had sent. It had been a few days since Chettan had started asking me to renew the rental agreement for his flat in Chennai, but I was too lazy to go.

However, this time, I felt a new-found enthusiasm to go and it definitely had a lot to do with the dream I had seen.

'Anyway, I must visit once to renew that rental agreement. If I make it this week, I can meet you too, right?' I texted her.

'Hey, that is fantastic! I have waited a year to get your signature on my copy of your book. Dude, I am so excited to meet you.'

'Me too!' I texted back.

I glanced up to see that thirty-three-year-old man with a serene expression on his face; it appeared as if he were smiling at me with his eyes. I needed answers from him.

'God, why did I see such a dream last night? She is a very decent girl. To this day, she has always maintained her integrity and has never once behaved questionably with me. None of our chats ever crossed the limit. Even then, why did all this happen in my dream? Is it that the desires that I had suppressed are manifesting as dreams? Anyway, I am going to Chennai ... What say?'

On the altar, an open Bible lay. I picked it up.

It was open on Mathew 4:1-11: 'Then Jesus was led by the Spirit into the wilderness to be tempted by the devil. After fasting forty days and forty nights, he was hungry. The tempter came to him and said, "If you are the Son of God, tell these stones to become bread."'

MISSED BY A HAIR

'Nail the basics first, detail the details later.'

—CHRIS ANDERSON, owner of TED, Technology, Entertainment and Design

Andre Agassi, the tennis phenomenon who won eight Grand Slam titles, was an icon of the sport in the 1980s, much like Roger Federer is today. Agassi's long, golden hair became a craze among young men and women. In 1990, during his first Grand Slam final, the whole world was watching the twenty-year-old with hope. However, he lost without putting up a good fight, much to everyone's disappointment. He revealed in his 2009 autobiography, *Open*, the cause of his defeat: 'I wore a wig, and it cost me the French Open.' The truth was that his long hair was actually a wig! On the day before the finals, his wig began to come loose. Petrified at the thought of the world discovering the fact the next day, Agassi chose to use a clip given to him by his brother to secure the wig in place. His preoccupation with his hair ultimately led to his defeat.

Returning from work, I had just stepped off the bus at Angamaly when I remembered the 'serious warning' Amma had given me that morning.

'Today, you will not be allowed back into the house until you get a haircut. Furthermore, you cannot accompany me to the wedding tomorrow without having your hair properly done,' she had proclaimed.

I was grown up and well employed, but none of that ever made a difference to her. She still dealt with me like an errant schoolboy who needed meticulous supervision. The daughter of a teacher who had once worked with Amma was getting married the next day. It was a chance to meet the children of all the teachers together. Amma was very particular about me looking handsome when we arrived. When I was a little boy, she would take me to her school's annual function. Even back then, she insisted that I wear the nicest clothes to ensure I looked suave.

'What will I get by dressing up so much or looking very good?' I wanted to ask. But then I decided that getting a haircut was much easier than convincing Amma that beauty is skin deep, considering she applied sunscreen every night before bed.

'Which barbershop would be open at this time?' I wondered. It was 8.20 p.m. I had already bitten off and spit out parts of my nails, and it seemed like the beginning of a 'prolonged inconclusive contemplation about the subject', but then, at a distance, I saw a sparkling name board with red letters on it.

'VARSHA BEAUTY PARLOUR'.

The name sounded very familiar; I had heard this name in some context, but I simply couldn't place it. And then, within seconds, a few flashbacks rushed into my brain from out of nowhere and clarity began to dawn.

This barbershop, Varsha, had a 'marriage-oriented' history with our family. On days before their respective marriages, my elder brothers had their hair done at Varsha. On the face of it, this salon specialized in the 'Manavalan cut', that monotonous haircut that most bridegrooms were found to surrender to. At the Carnival Movie House in Angamaly, the Varsha Beauty Parlour promo came after that disgusting anti-tobacco advertisement we're all familiar with.

To cut a long story short, this place was famous.

Finding another salon open at that time of the night would be a rarity, so I decided to take the chance. I walked towards Varsha, curious to see how they do their hairdo.

The 'Open' sign outside made me happy. An enthusiastic air conditioner chilled my sweaty skin as I entered, its air almost tickling me. It was my first time inside an air-conditioned salon.

'Welcome, sir.'

A neatly dressed Bengali lad stood at the door and greeted me. Even that was a first for me: A salon employee dressed as well as or even better than the customer. And despite being Bengali, he had that 'Keralite air' about him.

When I walked in, I was amazed. It wasn't just another barbershop. The decor could easily be mistaken for a luxury hotel.

Let me elaborate a bit.

The air conditioning was centralized, far ahead of its time and beyond the advancement of the locality. There was an enormous high-definition TV in the centre. The walls were covered with numerous mirrors, creating the impact of a maze. It resembled the room to which the villain escapes from Bruce Lee in the climax of *Enter the Dragon*. Everywhere I looked, I only saw myself. There was a luxurious, yet cozy-looking sofa set. Music was playing from all sides. Two redundant ceiling fans stood motionless on the ceiling, almost as if that stillness was their protest.

When I finished gawping at the room, I turned around to find another guy standing right in front of me. He bore an uncanny resemblance to the first guy; they must be brothers or at least cousins, I reckoned.

'Sir, shall we go for a hair wash?' he asked me with a smile.

He politely took my bag and placed it on a shelf. I hadn't experienced such hospitality before.

'Please follow me, sir. Hair wash is done in the next room.'

I followed him, lost in my thoughts. The ritual of washing my hair before getting a haircut was new. At Shivan Chettan's barbershop, where I had been getting my haircut ever since hair first emerged on my head, the haircut was a completely different affair. With Shivan Chettan, it was a blink-and-you-miss-it process. You'd sit on the chair, blink once and your haircut would be done. Moreover, washing your hair after the haircut made more sense, so why wash it before? My mind was busy.

'Sir, you may recline on the sofa and close your eyes,' he said. The sofa resembled a dentist's chair but had a spotless white washbasin in place of a headrest. I lay down, positioning my head correctly in the washbasin—an apparatus I believed was meant only for hands or mouths. Keeping my head in a washbasin was a first again.

What he did next seemed a bit extreme to me as a Christian. He covered my face with a white cloth! In our Christian tradition, we cover the face of the deceased before lowering them into the grave.

'Hey, what's going on, man?' I scowled at him.

'It is to keep the soap off your eyes and face, sir,' he replied earnestly.

Afterwards, he massaged a few substances into my hair and scalp. This brought back memories of the Rasnadi Choornam my mother used to apply to my head when I was a child. He washed my hair with lukewarm water, not forgetting to gently massage my scalp during the wash. I have to admit this: It felt terrific!

'Sir, now you can sit up straight,' he said. When I did, he started to dry my hair with a well-laundered, fragrant Turkish towel.

When I thought of that guy, who should have been around my age, doing all these services, my mind started to sympathize with him, quite unnecessarily. Even though I told him I would do the drying myself, he didn't allow me to. Also, the way he moved the towel had something special to it: A rhythm, a tempo.

Actor Nivin Pauly's celebrated line from the blockbuster movie *Thattathin Marayathu* came to my mind, but with 'towel drying' squeezed into it.

'Even though my hair was towel-dried many times before, it is for the first time that towel-drying felt like a miracle!'

That was how marvellously he towel-dried my hair.

'Sir, now we shall go to the cabin for haircutting?'

He led me into the room and gestured for me to enter first. The room was impressive; everything I saw there amazed me. In one corner, there was a plasma TV playing MTV; two powerful speakers were positioned on opposite walls. A large and beautiful mirror adorned one side of the room. Talcum powders and colognes from different brands were neatly arranged in a row, resembling an identification parade. Trimmers and blades of various specifications and power were displayed on another table, reminding me of the weapons exhibited after being seized from terrorist groups who had surrendered to the law.

'With so much arms and ammunition, this haircut is going to be kickass,' my subconscious whispered as I sat in the chair. The hairstylist came and stood behind me. He ran his fingers through my hair to ensure it was dry enough to be cut. He expertly flicked away some water drops that wouldn't leave, as if he were playing a break shot on a carrom board.

'Shall we maintain your existing hairstyle, sir?' he asked.

Shivan Chettan never gave you any choices. The only choice you could make was whether to go into his barbershop or not. So, when asked about a preferred hairstyle, I didn't know what a good reply would be.

'I'd like a hairstyle that is trendy right now, but not very cheeky,' I replied with a smile.

He pressed a button on the chair and it started to ascend, taking me to a comfortable height for him. After witnessing all of this, one thing was clear: My wallet would be lighter of at least Rs 500 when I left this place. That was downright extravagant compared to Shivan Chettan's humble remuneration.

'In the front, we shall do a bit of spike,' he proposed.

'We may,' I agreed.

Over here, the plot took a sharp twist, much like the interval scene of a movie.

After briefly leaving the room, the man returned holding a pair of hair-cutting scissors in one hand and a long, sharp, shiny screwdriver tightly gripped in the other. To say that I was horrified would be an understatement. It felt like his gaze was narrowing in on me. It was only the day before that I had read about Yavuz Yapıcıoğlu, the Turkish serial killer and arsonist nicknamed 'The Screwdriver Killer'. He came and stood right behind me. Unable to decide what could trigger a potential murderer, my mind searched for a good response. The screwdriver in his hand shone in the mirror.

'Brother, we don't need any fancy hairstyle. Are you planning to style the spike backward like they did in the movie *Boys* with … er … the screwdriver? I think something simpler would be enough.' I tried to sound as casual as possible. His reply made me breathe out a sigh of relief.

'Sir, the screwdriver is not for curling your hair. I keep it on hand because the screw in these scissors is loose. I must tighten it occasionally so it doesn't slip and accidentally hit your face,' he explained.

Knowing that the scissors could slip from your hairdresser's hand and maybe scratch your cheek was scary, but it was nothing compared to your hairdresser unmasking himself to be the screwdriver killer.

I was relieved.

The moment threat and fear were removed from the equation, human tendencies like sarcasm and satire began to resurface in me.

Once again, I looked at him and all around. The celebrated Varsha Beauty Parlour had everything: Centralized air conditioning, plasma TV, wall-mounted speakers, ten types of talcum powders, twenty brands of colognes, an apparatus to wash your hair and whatnot. But it didn't have a reliable pair of scissors.

'You don't have another pair of scissors?' I asked.

'This will do, sir; I have always used this one. I will manage,' he said in a tone that was the quintessence of confidence.

What was my opinion of him at that point? I had only two options to pick from: He was either crazy or he just appeared so to my eyes.

When I contemplated that this fancy barbershop lacked proper scissors, I almost decided to leave after expressing my disapproval. Yet, when I considered his innocent expression, I chose not to.

Thus, for the first time, I went through an entire haircut with my eyes wide open. My expression resembled a deer caught in headlights while crossing a forest path at night. I didn't mind seeing my reflection staring back at me in the mirror, as I needed to keep my eyes open to avoid being hurt if the scissors slipped from his hand. Secondly, I was tired after a long day at the office, so falling asleep during the haircut and seeing a nightmare about the screwdriver killer was also possible. I didn't fancy that either.

Finally, when it was done, he charged me only Rs 200 for cutting my hair without any major calamities.

While paying him, I decided to give him a piece of advice: 'Dude, customers don't come here to watch television, enjoy music or appreciate the air conditioning. Not primarily, at least. They come to get a good haircut. So please do get a pair of reliable scissors. Just because Mayflower Hospital is nearby, don't attempt life-threatening haircuts every day of the week.'

From how things had gone so far, I expected him to respond with a 'No, sir, Tuesday is a holiday'. But he didn't.

'When you come for your next haircut, I promise you will see brand-new scissors, sir,' he said, trying to conceal his embarrassment unsuccessfully.

'See, this conviction you have is your success. And, of course, this smile of yours.' I patted his back and left.

He stood there smiling.

Once I got home that day, I narrated my haircut escapade to Appan and Amma. They laughed heartily. After Amma laughed to exhaustion, she said something I'll share here for you to ponder.

'There are certain good things that others expect from us. If we fail at providing those, no matter what else we do, whatever circus we put on, they won't value us. Be it hairdressing, be it life.'

What say?

XX AND XY

'Why are women … so much more interesting to men than men are to women?'

—VIRGINIA WOOLF

I was a young boy at the time. We were all watching the song 'Pranayamanithooval' from the movie *Azhakiya Ravanan* on Doordarshan's *Chithra Geetham*. That's when my mother commented, 'They say a woman's body is God's most beautiful creation. Bhanupriya, as an actress, has a great, shapely physique. She is so beautiful.' Now that I've grown up, I can confidently say that the female body is the greatest masterpiece of God, the craftsman. I recently watched a speech by Cameron Russell, the American model, on YouTube. The title of her talk was 'Looks aren't everything. Believe me, I am a model'. She discussed the insecurities that come with beauty and how being constantly objectified can be burdensome for women.

In 2017, there was a significant surge in female empowerment movements on global media platforms. The #MeToo campaign, in which women shared their experiences of sexual harassment, had a profound impact. A tweet by Hollywood actress Alyssa Milano on 16 October 2017 revitalized the #MeToo movement, originally started ten years earlier by Tarana Burke, an African-American woman. This brought global attention to the movement.

Alyssa Milano wrote: 'If you've been sexually harassed or assaulted, write "me too" as a reply to this tweet.'

The #MeToo movement had a strong impact in Kerala, where thousands of women used social media platforms like Facebook to share their stories of harassment. Prominent figures such as Sajitha Madathil and Rima Kallingal also shared their experiences. Naturally, many pointed fingers at men, questioning why they let lust overpower them to such an extent. This led me to do a lot of reading and thinking, and have numerous discussions with both male and female friends. Everyone had their own opinion, each with its merits and drawbacks, but the one common thread was a lack of clarity in understanding the issue.

Being a man representing the demographic that ignited the #MeToo movement, I want to express some thoughts. This is not an effort to justify, but rather an acknowledgment. You may disregard it with contempt or perceive it as a man's confession and attempt to understand, if not forgive. There is something inherently wrong with the way men, including myself, are wired by God.

When it was just the two of us in an elevator, I asked the girl who was my first love if I could kiss her on her lips. The request was driven by the physical urge of the moment. This was her reply: 'I am scared, Joseph. I am not scared of kissing you. But if we do that and you quarrel with me sometime after, it will hurt me a hundred times more than it does now.' I had been thinking a lot about the reasoning behind her response. We were in love and had kissed one another, but why did our arguments or my harsh words affect her more after the kiss? When a girl lets a guy kiss her in the name of love, is there something deeper going on within her beyond the kiss? And for him, is the experience just a transaction of pleasure through the lips?

I have encountered many girls who have broken down, saying that they have willingly been physically intimate with someone because of their love for him. But I have never met a guy who cried about being physically intimate with a woman he loved. Why is this so? For a man, why isn't his physicality as intimate? Why does a girl desire deep conversation and affection after intimacy, while the guy may casually join his friends for a movie?

It is tempting to think that men have an irreversible overdose of lust due to hormonal differences. Moreover, societal influences have further contributed to this, leading to the development of certain behaviours in men. I can sense some women reading this beginning to get infuriated.

'Hey, you can't hide behind your hormones. Please grow up,' I can hear them say. As I mentioned, this is just an attempt to acknowledge some doubts and questions.

Shall we look at this from a different direction?

The concept of a girl's virginity, chastity and purity has always been emphasized as she grows up. While this may not be true for everyone, it is undoubtedly the case for many girls growing up in an average household. When a girl allows a man to touch her body, is it solely due to mutual heterosexual attraction or is she giving him access to elements she has protected throughout her life? Is this why she is so affected, or does it have nothing to do with her body?

Travelling on public buses can be uncomfortable for many girls. Even a single unwanted touch can cause distress. I have heard my friends share this. While travelling on a bus, even well-intentioned men may feel their bodies heating up if a woman stands too close. Why could that be? Wait a second if you are urged to say, 'Joseph, it is high time you consult a good doctor.'

How often have you experienced men glaring at you because your body accidentally touched theirs? Why don't we, as men, find these acts repulsive?

The most famous line from a Bollywood blockbuster comes to mind: 'Kuch kuch hota hai, tum nahi samjhoge'—which translates to 'Some things happen, you won't understand.' However, unlike in the movie, the subject we discuss here is not fictional but real. It's as real and disturbing as it can get. It's high time we all try to understand it.

Since childhood, I have had some questions that I always wanted answers to. I'm going to ask them now.

Why did my lower primary teacher ask only the girls to never straddle their seats?

When an actress was dancing on TV and close-up shots of her midriff were shown, my grandmother remarked, 'Aren't any of these women ashamed?' Then she turned to me, ten years old at the time, and commanded, 'Close your eyes, boy!' Why did my grandmother instruct me to close my eyes but didn't do the same to my sisters when a shirtless Salman Khan danced on screen, with just his guitar occasionally covering his upper body?

In Indian mythology, celestial female dancers were sent from the heavens to disturb the abstinence of saints during deep meditation. Why so?

Once, a trainer visited our school to improve our elocution skills. A line he said stayed with me as if etched in stone: 'A good speech should be like a woman's skirt: Long enough to cover the subject and short enough to create interest.' I wondered why it had to be so. Does biology make the female body more adept at creating attraction? Or is it that the male psyche projected it to such a dimension?

During the Kargil War, a popular hearsay emerged. It is said that a Pakistani soldier took a disrespectful dig at the Indian Army, saying, 'Give us Madhuri Dixit and we will give you Kashmir.' After the Indian Armed Forces defeated the Pakistani forces, they responded, 'To all of you, with love, from Madhuri Dixit.' Legends say that wars were fought to claim women. Women have been taken as hostages or used as stakes in gambling, dating back to ancient folklore.

When a girl reaches menarche, why do movies portray it as something to be shy or secretive about? Why is it depicted in ways that spark men's curiosity? Why is the female form consistently portrayed as endlessly captivating to us?

Why did comedy shows from our childhood make jokes about female body parts, like the navel, for instance, as if it were funny? After all, men also have navels!

I can't help but think that something has to change in the way boys are brought up. When so much attention is paid to raising girls, does a boy's upbringing receive that much supervision? As a child, I did not get one-fourth of the attention that the average girl around me received. I was never taught to look at girls like equals; instead, I was always instructed to watch against someone 'snatching or stealing' those precious beings. Which is why, in many places, men still tag along wherever a woman goes; his lifetime assignment is 'surveillance'.

I believe it's a basic human tendency to want to open something when somebody asks you to keep it closed. I think it's time we do away with phrases like 'if it was your mother' or 'if she was your sister', and instead use 'if it was you' and 'if it was something against your will'. The coming generations should be taught that when a man assaults a woman in a fit of emotions, it is not the woman who is 'disgraced' or 'stained', but it is the respect and honour of every other man on this planet that is harmed. When such actions occur, the freedom of a woman's life and the dignity of every man are challenged.

I believe that if laws had been stricter, they would have reduced the prevalence of such hashtags to some extent. However, that was not the case, as we were all born and raised in a society where none of those laws ever seemed that strict, at least in the manner they were brought into action.

If my mother had used Facebook, she would have probably used that hashtag. Every woman has a story. Speaking as a man, I want to apologize for how we have limited your freedom. At the same time, I respectfully acknowledge that we are not the sole ones to blame.

The great poet Sachidanandan's lines seem all relevant here,

> It was on the sixth day,
> that God made a mistake.
> On that day, he created a creature with lust but no love,
> Which prays without humility,
> And kills without hunger!

The presence of the term 'sex' has hindered open discussion of an important issue—sex education. However, it is the most effective long-term solution to the injustices women face in our society. We should provide clear explanations about the female and male bodies in our education system. Instead of viewing the body as a place for mere physical pleasure, it should be regarded as a sacred temple. Just as we teach moral science, we should also teach respect for bodily integrity. Additionally, we should emphasize that the term 'sex' is not just about pleasure, but fundamental to the existence of life on this planet.

Teach us that a real man loves and respects a woman. Teach us that even a casual touch without her permission is a violation. Teach us that a woman's navel symbolizes a mother's relationship with her child. I would love to say just one thing to every woman: If you give birth to a boy, raise him to become a great human being. Teach him that any touch without permission, without love, is wrong. Like a sacred utterance, say 'Thathvamasi', which means 'You are it' in his ears. Let him grow up respecting her body as he respects his own.

Dear God, let men and women switch lives for one day, if possible.

Let women understand how difficult it is to walk around this planet with smouldering urges waiting to catch fire any moment. Let us, men, understand the ocean of agony that she lives in just because she is a woman. May we know each other better. May we kiss each other with our hearts.

THE HEART FIELD

'A Guru is not someone who holds a torch for you.
He is the torch.'

—SADHGURU

That man with an unusual look and disposition came to meet me at the office. With his wide, bright eyes, braided hair and soft smile, it seemed the vestment could not contain him. Mostly, it was silence; at times, words spilled like music. When he was returning after his short visit, I noticed that he hadn't worn any footwear. Initially, I thought that he must have left them outside the office. Later, I understood that he had none. How naive are the assumptions of us commoners! He had removed his slippers outside of Earth. Here is a man who removed his footwear in Heaven before stepping on this Earth with his right foot. He considered the whole Earth a temple; how could he step on it with his footwear?

—SUBASH CHANDRAN, IN THE FOREWORD OF *ORDINARY*

There is a lovely haiku penned by T.P. Rajeevan, author of the much-celebrated novel *Paleri Manikkyam*.

All the ways,
I lost so far,
Had been to you.

This is a beautiful line with infinite layers of meaning. Some may think that the poet expressed his version of an old spiritual idea: That all the times we cried and worried about having lost our way, about being on the wrong road, invariably, each one led to the ultimate destination. I am not sure if that is what he meant. But then again, it is said that every piece of writing has two meanings: What the writer meant and what the reader interpreted. Two people may understand the same line in two distinct ways.

This chapter delves into the influence of one particular writer who inspired me to read more and introduced me to a new level of literary enjoyment. After completing my Class Ten exams, I decided to enrol in the seminary. Or, as they say, the force that leads someone down many wrong paths to arrive at the right destination made that decision for me.

The desire to become a priest didn't arise naturally; it stemmed from an unusual flashback. Let's take a closer look and be right back.

When I was a young schoolboy, on the way from our school to her house, I used to amaze my first crush, Jisha Peter, by narrating my exaggerated versions of *The Jungle Book* episodes to her. One day, as usual, after captivating her with my stories, we parted ways at the junction to go to our respective homes. The tiny lover in me felt proud for making her laugh more than usual. Then I continued my walk home, asking plants if they had done their homework and whacking those lamp posts that failed to answer my questions from the previous day's lesson.

When I finally arrived at my house, I noticed a red Maruti Esteem car parked in front. Back then, only relatively well-off people owned such vehicles. As I approached the house, a balding man asked me if anyone was home. I opened the door taking the keys from where generations of this land had hidden their house keys, under the flower pot.

'Appan and Amma will be home soon. Who are you? And what do you want?' I asked, trying my best to convey the seriousness typically seen in elders at home.

'I am Bishop Thomas Chakkyeth's driver. At the moment, Father Thomas is at your neighbour Father Joseph Parekkatti's house; he will be here soon,' he replied.

Appan was always close to the church council and had warm relationships with many priests. I had often heard him mention Father Chakkyeth's name in our house. The reverence for the clergy that was passed down to me genetically began to bloom within me.

'Please come inside; Appan will come soon.'

I had barely finished speaking, when, to my alarm, Father Chakkyeth, accompanied by another priest I couldn't recognize and a nun I had seen a couple of times at church, walked in together.

'Are you Jose's second son? When will your Appan come?' Father Chakkyeth asked affectionately.

'I am the third. Appan will arrive soon. Father, please come inside and take a seat.' I tried to sound as courteous as I possibly could. As they entered, they smiled at the hospitality of a third-standard child. I felt overwhelmed; it seemed as if a huge responsibility was on my shoulders. I found myself resorting to the clichéd line my mother always used whenever we had visitors.

'I shall get something to drink.'

I must admit I hadn't thought much about the implications of a possible positive response to this proposal.

'Of course, sure. I can't wait to see what you get us to drink,' the Father said. In hindsight, the Father didn't look all that thirsty; he must have just intended to sweetly encourage a little boy's enthusiasm. Whatever it was, I had reached the point of no return. But I was not worried at all. I knew where all the snacks were kept; all I had to do was grab some and serve them on plates.

I ran to the kitchen and searched all the containers and boxes that always held biscuits, snacks or achappam. And what did I find?

Praise the lord, nothing!

That was okay—the refrigerator was always there to come to the rescue. At any given day, it would have some fruit—apples, oranges or something or the other. But on that eventful day, all of them had magically vanished! I could only find a glass bowl with partially solidified fish curry from last night. In retrospect, its shape reminded me of the glacier that hit the *Titanic*. That was when I noticed a packet of sliced milk bread in a compartment on the fridge's door! Columbus finding what he thought was India or me finding the milk bread—who was more ecstatic? I don't have an answer to date. But I didn't have enough time to dwell on that happiness; I had to find something the guests could drink. My eyes wandered the horizons of our kitchen.

Mister Butler Soda Maker—we had one of those! It stood right on the kitchen counter, ready to oblige. Unlike today, not many homes had a soda maker back then. As a child, you were lucky if your parents decided to buy one for your home. Even if your family was poor, owning a Mister Butler Soda Maker made you feel rich. Yes, if one affordable item could make a poor man feel wealthy, it would be the soda maker. It doesn't make sense, but those were the times.

I climbed up on the stool and made a bottle of soda.

I confidently entered the main hall, holding a bottle of soda in my right hand and a plate of four shivering slices of bread in my left hand. Our soda maker only produced one small bottle at a time. I handed that bottle of soda to the Father and then offered him the plate of bread so he could pick the cold slice of his choice. I remember noticing the other guests covering their mouths with their palms and I presumed they were containing their admiration—but now I realize they were trying to handle their shock. Stifling a laugh, the bishop took the bottle of soda with his left hand and a slice of bread with his right. To this day, I believe that the bishop was the first homo sapien to ingest chilled bread with soda in human evolutionary history.

Since I had brought out only one bottle of soda, I felt the need to appease the other guests.

'You all will get yours. As soon as Father drinks his soda and returns the bottle, I shall make the next.' That proclamation would have put the bishop under tremendous pressure.

'Son, we don't need soda; we will just have bread!' They sounded convincing, but they were still laughing while taking their slices.

Then, like music, I heard the sound of Appan's Yamaha RX 100 bike.

'Appan has arrived,' I announced.

As soon as he walked in, Appan saw the bishop tackling the soda and bread he was pitted against. The others gaped at their only predicament, the bread. One would be justified to say that their stares looked 'cold breaded'. They resembled those unfortunate people who get odd food combinations at makeshift refugee camps. If Appan were Gen-Z, he would have certainly said, 'Big yikes!' out loud. He didn't do that, but the expression on his face superseded anything he could have verbalized.

Very soon, Amma also returned from school. The bread and soda were instantly removed from the teapoy and replaced with fresh cups of tea and a plate of salted cashew nuts. From there, normalcy returned to the scene, and the elders conversed about the world. When they got up to leave, Bishop Thomas Chakkyeth did something that changed my life forever.

With a lot of fondness, he held me close and said to Appan, 'He is very smart. Jose, you have three sons. Why don't you give him to us?'

The nun gazed at my mother with an expression that seemed to imply, 'Doesn't that resemble God's call?'

Over time, the idea went through rounds and rounds of discussion. Whenever or wherever they caught a glimpse of me, the nuns reminded me of what the bishop had said. They would tell me to prepare myself well.

I joined the seminary right after completing my Class Ten exams. Even today, when someone probes as to why I joined the seminary, I still have only one answer: 'A lot of people told me a lot of things, and a lot of it I believed. When I chose that path, it had to do with all of it.'

After joining the seminary, I realized that nothing was more valuable than one's freedom. I had run around and laughed all my life until then, but I had now surrendered myself to a life governed by many rules and the timely bong of the church bell. At the seminary, we had classes held on different subjects, such as the Bible, English and music. With a lot of effort, I started to learn to love that life. Then, one day, Father Kuriakose Puthenmaanayil, who was in charge of us, told us about a new class that a new Father, Bobby Jose Kattikkad, would teach the next day. Already feeling overwhelmed by the monotony of classes held by numerous Fathers and nuns, the idea of a 'new Father' didn't sound all that new.

The next day, a young Father with long hair and a beard walked into our class barefoot! He spoke in a very tranquil manner. His speech didn't have the power to captivate the audience. On the contrary, it often sounded boring and could even make you very sleepy. His speech was slow, his voice was low and his rhythm was repetitive. We were asked to write down everything he said—not just the main points but literally every word that came out of his mouth. So it was natural that my hands hurt after his class. Sometimes, I would pretend to write notes but not take anything down really.

We only had his classes for a few short months. On one of the days, we learnt that Father Bobby had written a book and that it was coming out the next day. The building's notice board said the book would be available for seminary students at a discounted price. This was Father Bobby's second book and was proofread by the man in charge of us at the seminary, Father Kuriakose Puthenmaanayil. It was this fact that prompted many of us to buy a copy of it—the purchase was intended to please the Father in charge of us and it had nothing to do with the book itself. Thus, for the first time, I bought a book myself and paid for it. The book's name was *Hridayavayal*, which meant 'the heart field'.

The book's front cover featured a still from a film about St. Francis of Assisi, showing the main character, Francis, and his friends. The back cover had a picture of the author, Father Bobby, which piqued my interest. It was the first time I had encountered a book written by someone I had met in person, which gave me a reason to like it. During our study time, I opened the book to write my name on the front page. Among us, writing one's name on the front page of a book in the most aesthetically pleasing way possible was considered an art form in itself and a sure way to kill time. While doing this, I noticed a small note on that page. It went like this:

> Dedication:
>
> To my father, who convinced me that books were better than toys,
> To my spiritual friends who serve me the supper of love that I am undeserving of,
> And lastly, you, who remind me that nothing written ever goes to waste.

That last line attracted me a lot—lastly, you, who remind me that nothing written ever goes to waste.

It seemed as if it had been written for me and spoken directly to me. That's where my journey into the world of reading began. I started realizing that the wrong paths were leading me to something right. When I ventured into the world of literature accompanied by the words of a wise man, it opened up the enchanting universe of books for me.

The Father wrote, 'When a beggar who got food from a certain house directs another beggar to that house, that is the real gospel.'

When Father Bobby described Christ as the 'young, thirty-three-year-old woodworker', the man whom, until that point, I had only acknowledged as Lord Jesus, started looking like a friend.

'Spirituality is like awakening your nostalgia. Think about when you were a child walking through a festival. How beautiful were the balloons, toys and drumbeats? But then, at some point, the child loses his father's fingertip. After that, the wonderful things he encounters no longer make him happy; instead, they frighten him.'

When he wrote that spirituality is walking forward holding the fingertip of your father, the Almighty, I began to comprehend the real meaning of the prayer, which says, 'Our Father, who art in heaven.' Tears filled my eyes when Father Bobby wrote that God is not in heaven but amidst us.

Gradually, I began to understand that capacious love was the cornerstone of spirituality. On the little blank spaces between the pages of Father Bobby's book, I scribbled some of my thoughts for the first time, noting down the things I understood when I read the book.

When the Father said that celibacy was not superior to married life and that spiritual pursuits begin when you start asking yourself questions, I asked myself the first question.

'Do I have the true desire to become a priest?'

The answer I received from within was no. When I realized that God was present in our search for Him and that wearing a priest's vestment was unnecessary for a spiritual seeker, I heard the true calling from the one I had previously believed had called me.

I then left the seminary.

Later, I was transplanted to Bangalore. Amidst unprecedented pleasures, a single spark ignited within me by the Father began to guide me, even though I was unaware of it. I roamed around in search of new books by him.

Although he is a Christian priest, his writing often references the Mahabharata, the Ramayana, the Quran and Buddhist literature.

He also incorporates elements from Malayalam movies such as *Kammattippaadam*, *Ozhimuri* and *Pranchiyettan & the Saint*, as well as foreign movies like *The Bicycle Thief* and *Children of Heaven*.

In the Father's writing, I first learned about a set of books that a person should read in their lifetime. The books included Dostoevsky's *The Brothers Karamazov*, O.V. Vijayan's *Kadaltheerathu*, Nikos Kazantzakis's *Francis*, Khaled Hosseini's *A Thousand Splendid Suns*, Gabriel García Márquez's *One Hundred Years of Solitude* and Paulo Coelho's *The Alchemist*. I sought out these books because the Father had introduced them to me with love.

I have always been drawn to the confessional. Father Bobby re-introduced it to me as a safe space, a friend I could always turn to. It wasn't a place to stand burdened by guilt, but a place that listened silently, offering unconditional forgiveness and never making you feel ashamed.

I was like a child responding eagerly to the bell of an ice cream cart; I bought and read every book the Father wrote as soon as they were released. Additionally, I tried to seek out and read all the books mentioned by him in his works. The Father's writing had a magical quality—it seemed as if his words were infused with the power of love that inspired readers to write. Writing my autobiography, I transitioned from the world of reading into the realm of writing.

At the age of twenty-seven, I wrote my first book. The first line of the first chapter was from the Father's book, *Nilathezhuthu*. It read, 'Nothing is lost until you rediscover it.'

While documenting my life experiences, I viewed the world through the Father's perspective. Even my failures displayed a spiritual undercurrent when seen through his lens of love, forgiveness and hope.

Today, I am best known for my videos on Facebook and YouTube. People often say that my unique way of thinking and words inspire them. The question I frequently receive in personal messages or on Facebook comments is, 'Who has inspired you the most?' Without hesitation, I can say that the person who has inspired me the most is the Capuchin priest, Father Bobby Jose Kattikkad.

Years later, I was fortunate enough to meet him in person once again. I fell silent before his calm, graceful smile, unable to articulate my thoughts. As we parted ways, I shared my inner turmoil with him: 'Father Bobby, my life is a constant battle. On the outside, I am a youngster people look to with hope, a motivational speaker whom people wish to meet. But most of the time, I grapple with deep complexities and weaknesses of my own.'

'Joseph, create good surroundings for yourself,' he replied before walking away.

That night, I watched a programme called *Gurucharanam* on Shalom TV. In it, the Father mentioned something called the 'church bell syndrome'. According to him, some people are like church bells. What is unique about a church bell? It makes noise and summons people to the church. Whether righteous or wicked, honest or deceitful, they heed the call of the church bell and enter the church. However, ironically, the church bell always remains outside the church. What Father said was right; it could be that some people's calling is to be such church bells. Their destiny could be to bravely be the voice of good, even while remaining outside of it.

Beloved Father Bobby, I wish to recall your words.

'And lastly, you, who remind me that nothing written ever goes to waste.'

Yes, your words have not gone in vain. From what you have written, a church bell has sprung into existence. And I am that church bell! Please pray for me so that I can continue to make noise until the day the rope breaks and I fall.

> May footsteps be circumambulations,
> May the body be a shrine,
> May sorrows be flowers for worship,
> And words be sacred chants.

THE SOUL OF A STREETLIGHT

'If I could give you one thing in life, I would give you the ability to see yourself through my eyes. Only then will you realize how special you are to me.'

—UNKNOWN

Once, Jude Anthany Joseph, the young filmmaker known for his movie *Om Shanthi Oshana*, came to our church to participate in the inauguration ceremony of KYCM, the church's youth forum. When he spoke that day, he shared something worth remembering.

'I didn't gain anything outstanding from catechism classes, but I still remember something a teacher of mine told me when I was young. I had found a ten rupee note on the road with no one to claim it. I asked my teacher what I should do with it. She said, "Son, you may keep seven rupees for yourself. With three, you should buy candies for your friends. God blesses you with ten rupees to share three with someone else."'

What ten years of catechism classes couldn't teach him about how to live life, that teacher could in a minute. What we need is not preaching but great examples, period!

'Joseph, I request you to please talk to my son. He is very adamant and short-tempered, and won't move an inch regardless of how much his teachers or I advise him. I have watched your videos, so I felt that maybe he would receive it better if you spoke to him. These days, kids seem to listen only to youngsters.'

That was the message I received in my Facebook inbox.

'Chechi, I am facing a similar situation myself. I argue with my mother the most and it's a flaw in my personality that I've been trying to change for years without success. I don't think I can make your son understand,' I wrote back to her.

'Please don't say that, son. I have sought your help after intense prayers. Please consider this as a mother's request. We stay at Edappally. You can let me know a place and time that would be convenient for you, and I will send him. I would have loved to accompany him, but I am choosing not to, as there's a chance that he won't open up in my presence.'

I thought for a few moments before composing my response.

'I want to be honest; I'm unsure if I can make him understand. But, in any case, I will listen to him. I shall also speak with him for a bit. Please ask him to meet me at the Lulu Mall food court at 11.30 a.m., in front of the Baskin-Robbins outlet tomorrow.'

I gave her my contact number.

The following day, I met the boy and we had a conversation. He was a talented lad. He could draw, sing and play the guitar well. He had a budding music band of his own. His mother, a bank manager, and his father, a college dean, considered his music band activities to be 'cheap'. Their son wasn't meeting their academic expectations. And what was their expectation? That he should be the class topper. They constantly pressed him to drop his musical pursuits and focus exclusively on his curriculum.

How could he not be mad at his mom and dad? When he sat before me, I could see the roots of his anger. For a moment, I seriously considered changing sides and advising his parents on his behalf instead, but then I decided against that enterprise.

'You should never drop music, no matter what!' I told him. 'At the same time, you should try not to piss off your parents either. Put more effort into your studies—even if it is just for their sake. You can be good at both; they should realize that music is your passion. Do you know something? A.R. Rahman wanted to be an electronics engineer! It was his mother who wanted him to be a musician. Maybe we have today's Rahman because he heeded his mother to an extent. I am trying to say that these conflicts happen everywhere and there are constructive ways to deal with them. Give weightage to the wishes of your parents too. Once you become both an academic success and a musical hitmaker, try telling them you are dropping music. I bet they will call me again to advise you against quitting music; we know how parents are, right!'

I saw him laugh a bit for the first time. If I had to earn his trust, I had to hold on to that mood.

'You think they will have a problem saying that their son is a great student and a rockstar? But for them to be able to cherish the rockstar part, we must take away their worry about the student. We need all of it, man, and you know what? We can have all of it! And here is a bonus: Don't ask me how, but your academic efforts will someday help you surprisingly in unexpected areas of music. So, from now on, twist the throttle on both.'

His face just lit up.

'Shall we eat something before dispersing? What would you like to have?' I asked him.

'Oh, no, brother. You need to tell me what you would prefer to have! Mom has told me that, if possible, we should have lunch together. And I have strict instructions that I must not let you pay. She has given me money for it.'

That was when I noticed a rolled 2000 rupee note in his fist.

A young chap with a currency note in his hand and a Baskin-Robbins stall in the background—that image was more than enough to remind me of Deepu Chettan. Why? Years earlier, I had stood precisely like this boy against a similar backdrop.

It is a not-so-boring flashback, if a bit lengthy though. But it won't wear you down.

It was my elder brother Arun's wish for me to study at Christ College in Bangalore rather than my own. My life changed significantly during my time at Christ, mainly due to a special type of friendship that was new to me. I was embraced by a tight-knit group of friends, which included Deepu, Anand, Sally and Arun. Despite Arun being my actual brother, all of them treated me like their younger sibling, showing me love and including me in their activities.

Every week, we used to dine out at a restaurant. Not once did I witness a debate about who would pay the bill. However, I noticed that Deepu Chettan always volunteered to pay first. Initially, I assumed he did so because he earned the highest salary among the four. After living with them for three years, I realized I was mistaken. Even now, though I am well-employed and earning good money, when I visit Bangalore and we go out to eat, Deepu Chettan still happily offers to pay for me. There is no particular reason for it; that is just how that man is.

When I was in Bangalore, Arun took care of all my expenses. Even though Arun never hesitated to give me money, since I received constant cues from my parents against wasting my older brother's money, I was really, really miserly. Once a friend even made a sarcastic comment, 'He monitors his money and holds on to it like a monitor lizard!'

One Sunday, I got a call from Deepu Chettan.

'Boy, have you visited the church?'

'No, Deepu Chetta. I was planning to go to St. Anthony's Church in the evening to attend the Holy Mass in English.'

'If you shower and get ready quickly, we shall go to the Infant Jesus Church.'

'Where is that? Shall we take the bike?'

'We needn't. It's just within walking distance.'

'Cool then. I will be right there.'

When we met, he told me that the Infant Jesus Church was 5 kilometres away. Yes, that was Deepu Chettan's idea of walking distance. I felt like I had walked into a trap. It was December and it was cold. We walked on, drawing our jackets tightly against the cold. During the walk, he asked about tidings from my college, and introduced me to important places and landmarks we saw on our way. He mentioned that the church we were going to was famous in the area, Vivek Nagar, and would be very crowded on Thursdays. It was believed that miracles happened there on those days. Nothing was unattainable if someone lit a candle before infant Jesus and prayed on a Thursday, he told me. Deepu Chettan kept talking and I didn't realize time was passing. As we were about to reach the church, I noticed a Baskin-Robbins outlet near it.

'Deepu Chetta, the ice cream prices here are exorbitant, right?'

'It is not that expensive …'

'At Christ, Baskin-Robbins is where the rich give treats. Back home, Uncle John's ice cream was just ten rupees. These are 150 or so!' I told him.

Deepu Chettan just nodded in response.

When we reached the church, I realized the Holy Mass was in Tamil. 'But Chetta, this is Tamil,' I protested.

He responded, 'So what? Prayer has no language. Every language is equally good when you utter a prayer in it.'

I agreed. We chose a bench in a less crowded area and kneeled. I closed my eyes.

Tamil is beautiful, but because I barely knew the language back then, lines of prayer that I had only heard in Malayalam or English until then sounded very strange when I heard them in Tamil. Blame it on my unfamiliarity with the poetic Tamil vocabulary, but many phrases sounded like abuses when my brain replaced the exact words with their corresponding positioning in Malayalam. For example, 'Thanthai' means father in Tamil, as does 'Thantha' in Malayalam. But when the former is used in respectable contexts, in Malayalam, for some reason, 'Thantha' is used most frequently when someone is abusing another's father! Such dissimilarities in verbal implications were creating a comical commotion in my head. Deepu Chettan, who may not be proficient in Tamil, continued the prayers and songs confidently while I struggled not to laugh as I watched him.

I was pretty sure we would return in an auto rickshaw, but I was wrong. For those 5 kilometres we had to traverse back, Deepu Chettan chose to walk again! After walking a short distance, he told me we would have to cross the road.

'But this is the way we need to go, right?' I was confused.

'Come on, boy, let's have some ice cream before we resume walking,' he said, walking straight to the Baskin-Robbins store.

'Oh, no! Deepu Chetta, I swear I did not bring up the topic of this ice cream earlier to coax you into buying it for me. We really needn't buy such expensive ice cream now, especially in this cold weather!'

Did Deepu Chettan think that our conversation about Baskin-Robbins was something I planted smartly to prompt him into buying me some? I was feeling very embarrassed.

'Joseph, these are all small wishes. We should fulfil them right away. Tomorrow, when you land a great job or have plenty of money, what if you are on a sugar-restricted diet? Or what if you don't like ice creams by then? So, such things are never for later. Come, I shall show you the flavours here.' His tone was very matter of fact.

That day, I had chocolate ice cream—maybe the most delicious chocolate ice cream I had ever had until then. We resumed walking. After eating our lunch at a Malayali restaurant named Kairali, we returned home.

'By taking you for a walk, Deepu must have taken you for a ride!' Anandettan made fun of me when we met for tea in the evening.

'But it was fun ... A different kind of experience,' I said.

'That is because it is your first time ... When repeated, you will say it is a different "unkind" experience!' Anandettan laughed at his own joke.

He continued, 'Ask your brother how many kilometres Deepu has made him walk over the years.'

On 25 July 2008, all of us met for dinner at Van Milano, an Italian restaurant in Koramangala. I remember the date precisely because earlier that day, a few mini bomb blasts at some bus stops had shocked the people of Bangalore. There were no casualties, thankfully.

News had flashed on TV that a terrorist group had claimed to be behind the incident. That day, after having chosen and ordered our starters, the blasts became our topic of discussion.

'Anyone who sets out to kill in the name of religion should be hanged!' When Anandettan made this statement, Arun and I agreed with him. But Deepu Chettan objected.

'Then how are we different from them? Both resort to manslaughter.'

And, as usual, the debate began—Deepu vs everyone!

'What kind of reasoning is that? Who they kill are innocent people! What do they gain from doing so? It is just wild fun for them!' Arun contested.

All I was doing was waiting for the starters to arrive. After all, a hungry man is least interested in bombs. Maybe the only bomb that could grab his attention was a keto-fat bomb.

'Arun, just imagine: What if you were denied a room, insulted by people or marginalized simply because of your religion? Wouldn't that eventually make you angry? Wouldn't you start to feel a desire for revenge if you were denied freedom or mistreated throughout your life for no fault of your own? I'm not trying to justify these miscreants, but these are the outbursts of the oppressed.'

'We already know that people who are too intelligent end up as radicals!' Arun tried to hold his fort with a barbed joke.

Deepu Chettan just laughed heartily.

'Let me throw some light on another outlook. When news comes out about a mother having clubbed her son to death, everyone thinks, "How could a mother do that!" What else can that mother do when he hurts her daughter, his sibling, as a sexual predator? Here, that mother needn't be vindicated, but even she deserves to be understood.'

Defusing the debate a bit, the starters arrived like divine intervention. When excellent food soon followed, we all swallowed our arguments as if they were dessert.

But even after we returned home, Arun's objections continued to boil. He ranted to me.

'What Deepu says is just absurd! Would he be sitting here dissecting outlooks if such mishaps happened to someone of his own?'

'You leave it now. Let us not go into the usual ritual of doing a post-mortem of every debate.' I threw water on his burning sense of justice.

The next day, during our English class at college, we had an exercise called 'critical evaluation'. We had to talk about some topic for five minutes. I was among the first ten roll numbers picked to speak. This was a part of an internal assessment, so marks were involved and I was tense. I talked about the blasts. I just repeated the various angles from which Deepu Chettan had attacked the issue the previous day.

When I finished, Professor Felix beckoned me to the front of the class. Putting his arm around my shoulders, he told the class, 'Now, this is proper critical evaluation; it is all about pointing out any differences that are particularly significant and evaluating them from different angles.' Instantly, I puffed out my chest to suggest this was nothing new to me and that I had been engaging in critical evaluation since I was a toddler.

I was an absolute failure in the first semester. My studies took a nose dive. Arun did not scold me; instead, he consoled me and suggested that everything would be fine if I studied harder the next time. Deepu Chettan learned that all I had managed was a second class. He took me to Serengeti restaurant on the top floor of Total Mall. He advised me: 'We believe you are serious about your academics, so we include you in all our activities. Your brother may not have reprimanded you about your poor grades; maybe he even consoled you, but let me tell you the truth. In times when you are supposed to study, you must study; there are no ifs or buts about that. What was your percentile in Class Twelve? 90! And now you have skied down to a pathetic second class. This is not acceptable. I would love to see a much better performance next time.'

That day, I did feel a bit sad and angry. But today, when I look back, I realize it was all Deepu Chettan's love in disguise.

Deepu Chettan read a lot. Once, he brought me a book, *The Goal*, and said, 'You should be reading all these. It has a lot of management lessons.' Did I read it then? No way. But an idea did breeze through me: If I ever read like him, then maybe I could think differently like him.

When we used to get together, we often played a game called 'Ashwamedham'. It is the name of a popular game show on Malayalam television and it's a kind of reverse quiz. The host, known as the grandmaster, G.S. Pradeep, would ask the day's guest twenty questions. Within those twenty questions, he would try to guess the name of the famous personality the guest had in mind. If the grandmaster failed, the guest won. *Ashwamedham* became so popular that it turned into a household game. Whenever our group played it, we would end up quarrelling!

When picking a name to be revealed with twenty questions, Arun, Anand and I would choose personalities like P.T. Usha, Pinarayi Vijayan or Bruce Lee—names that even those without admirable general knowledge are familiar with. But Deepu Chettan would choose an Urdu poet who lived among Afghan tribes or the Bangladesh finance minister who held the office for the shortest span!

After expending our twenty valuable questions and not finding the answer, we would ask Deepu Chettan to reveal it himself. And that's when our outrage would ignite. For example, he might say, 'Haven't you heard about the Sandbar Fight? Come on, guys, that was so easy! The answer is James Bowie, after whom the famous Bowie Knife is named!' For us, especially back then, the most lethal knife we had heard of, like many Keralites, was the Malappuram Knife! An iconic movie character, Professional Killer Pavanayi from *Nadodikkattu*, had made it famous. As you can guess, we were unfamiliar with the Bowie Knife or the American pioneer after whom it was named. But not Deepu Chettan; he seemed to know every human who had ever walked on earth.

'This is unfair! We are not playing with you anymore!' we would declare, exasperated. Then Arun, Anand and I would walk out to have tea. We have had countless 'teas of defeat'.

During that time, my brother got a six-month on-site assignment in London and he left. Meanwhile, Anandettan was in Kerala. Sally Chettan's wedding was approaching and he was busy with the arrangements. When Arun left Bangalore, I felt sad, but I knew I could easily overcome that feeling. On the day we saw Arun off while having dinner at the Mas Restaurant in Madiwala, Deepu Chettan said something softly, almost as if to himself. 'These guys who go for on-site jobs, which are supposedly six months long, never return in six months; they will stay there for at least a year, maybe even longer. Do you know how many opportunities of this kind were offered to me? I never opted for them because I didn't want to lose the happiness our group and our friendship gave me. But now I understand that not everyone feels that way. Maybe Anand will also leave for America very soon.'

In his eyes, I could see the sadness and seclusion of a man whose friends were leaving one by one.

Deepu Chettan was right. My brother returned only a year later. By then, Anandettan had left for the States and Sally Chettan had become a busy married man. Our group of five friends shrunk to a team of just two: Deepu Chettan and me. Deepu Chettan called me every morning. We would have breakfast at a restaurant; needless to say, he always paid. One day, before Deepu Chettan could take out his wallet, I gave the restaurant's cashier a 500 rupee note, which I had kept ready, rolled and hidden in my fist. The cashier took it and gave me the change. That day, Deepu Chettan scolded me for the first time.

'It is not a bad thing to have thought of paying. But right now, you are a student. When you go out to have food with Arun, your elder brother, would it be you who pays? For me, you are my younger brother. Paying for your food won't make me bankrupt! After all, it is food. Boy, money spent on buying someone food is never a loss. So, you needn't feel bad at all!'

Throughout the year, Deepu Chetan took care of my expenses whenever we were together. As my education in Bangalore was drawing to a close, Arun returned. Shalini Chechi entered Deepu Chetan's life. Shalini Chechi was an excellent addition to our group of friends. She was very good to me as well.

I returned to Kerala, concluding my life in Bangalore. Anand got married and so did Arun. I went on to complete my MBA and landed a job. The frequency of phone calls came down. Very rarely would all of us go on a trip. But the friendship remained as good as it was and didn't need frequent interaction to flourish.

I used to have a blog. After writing a lot online, I decided to stitch it all together into a book. That became my first book, *Buried*

Thoughts. On the day of the book launch, both of my brothers were out of the country. My eldest brother, Adarsh, was in Dubai and Arun was in Australia. They tried but couldn't manage to take a few days off to come down for the event.

I remember the day very clearly. It was a weekday, so many relatives had already asked to be excused from participating in the event, blaming their jobs. They had promised alternatives, such as coming home in the evening. Among the first ten people to arrive at the event on that inconvenient weekday was Deepu Chettan. The man, who held a senior managerial position at an IT company, took a day off from his busy work week to arrive early, just for me. After the launch, as I walked towards the podium to deliver the vote of thanks, I noticed Deepu Chettan sitting at the back in the last row. I still remember mentioning him in my speech.

'Today, for my book launch, I knew one thing for sure. Regardless of who would attend or not, I could always count on one person: My Deepu Chettan. Someone who cared for me like an elder brother right from the days I was in Bangalore. Deepu Chetta, would you mind standing up for a moment?' I requested from the dais.

The moment he stood up, everyone turned around. When they saw him standing in the last row, they acknowledged him with a big round of applause. But I know that for all the good he did for me, all the knowledge he imparted, the wisdom he shared and the love he never scrimped on, he deserves many more rounds of ovation and many more of many things good.

Beloved Deepu Chetta,

While I filled page after page with these reminiscences, I was sure that you also remember all of it as well as I do, if not better. I don't call you often and I have missed your birthday many times, but there is something you should know. I have always struggled to express this, but to me, you are nothing less than one of my own brothers!

Today, when I spoke to this boy who stood before Baskin-Robbins with money in his hand, the sentences I used were yours, the ones you told me. I am sure that tomorrow, when this young guy grows up to be a successful man, he will help another young boy with the same thoughts. The saying holds: Values are not taught but caught.

With love,
Joseph

THE MYSTIC RIVER

'Promises are worse than lies. You don't just make them believe, you also make them hope.'

—MARILYN MONROE

For me, 2018 started with a great movie, *Mayanadhi*. The love story of Appu and Mathan goes straight into the viewer's heart. Mathan's unfaltering love for Appu makes him return to her like a kitten, regardless of how often he is shooed away. Appu's unspoken love for Mathan strangely cradles her hope that Mathan will come back every time she has to drive him away. The movie ends with Appu waiting for Mathan, believing he will return someday. Only the heartbroken audience knows he cannot, and he will not, ever again.

'Sex is not a promise' is a quote from *Mayanadhi* that provoked a lot of discussion. In the movie's context, it meant that by making love with someone, you are not taking an oath to live the rest of your life with them. The fact that it was Appu, the female protagonist, who says this to Mathan after a beautiful night of making love caused a crack in the stereotype and sparked new conversations. Articles cropped up across social media, pointing the spotlight on an emerging perspective that sex need not be considered a life-altering event. Instead, it is an expression of love—beautiful in the moment but not a contract strong enough to bind two people for life. Many suggested that sex existed within the brackets of love. Once the brackets were closed, life could go on for both partners, unentangled with one another.

These debates summoned before me the face of a girl whose cry for help had popped up on my Facebook chat as a lengthy message on a random day, well past midnight. That text seemed to rumble, owing to some quietened voice underneath. Every word in it made an unsuccessful attempt to deadbolt a scream shoved deep down into its cellar.

Hi, Joseph, I don't know if you will read this. We are not even acquainted, so it is unclear to me why I feel like opening up to you. It could be out of the courage that comes from having nothing more to lose in life. I have watched a few of your videos and felt you speak honestly. I know, it could be just a feeling. 'Honesty' is a word I lost belief in long ago. But I am daring to trust once again.

I was born into a very regular family. The atmosphere at home was never very good. So, growing up, I found my happiness entirely in school and in my studies. Usually, parents tell their kids to study hard and excel, right? It never happened in my case. Still, doing well in academics was my only goal and a shortcut to happiness. I have been a law student in Delhi for the past three years. When I came to Delhi, I had only one thing on my mind. The good old 'study well and come out with flying colours' was my life's solo maxim. I stayed in the hostel. All my roommates had boyfriends. They talked to their lovers over the phone for hours. Some conversations went on from moon to sun, some from sun to moon. They would always tell me about their love lives. But not for once did I feel that my not having a boyfriend was a shortcoming. The situation back home had turned me into a horse with blinders on. Knowing it was entirely upon me to care for my younger sister never allowed me to think of anything besides my studies. All that while, my friends teased me about a guy from our class. 'The guy', really. Nearly every girl in our class had a liking for him—a true gentleman.

'He doesn't have a girlfriend, Deedi. We will work it out,' they would nudge me. Whenever I heard anything about him, it would invariably be good and positive. One day, he came up to me for a chat. While talking, he remarked that I seemed very silent and asked if life was entirely about studies for me. We spoke once in a while; they were just casual conversations, though—the kind any two classmates could have.

'How about we go and have tea together?' he asked me one day. I was not very keen to. But when he pressed, I agreed out of courtesy. That day, looking at me across that tea table, he had a glitter in his eyes. Before I could wonder if I was imagining things, he confessed he was in love with me. The moment caught me unawares. Even though he didn't let it show, I assumed he must have been equally nervous. He admitted that it was his first time expressing his love for someone.

'I am sorry,' I said, avoiding his proposal straight away. I, the horse with blinders on, did not have to reassess my priorities. Studies came first, and nothing else came anywhere close. But he accepted my response with a lot of respect. That is what set him a notch above everyone else; he always carried a distinctive dignity. We still met once in a while; we spoke sometimes. His love for me was always evident in everything he did.

My friends came to know that he had proposed to me. They almost started a campaign to convince me. 'Why do you look at love as something you should resist? He is a great guy. Romance is not a crime. You both even belong to the same community! His family is good too. You should never look down upon someone's true love!'

By then, somewhere within, I had also started loving him. No, I started expressing the love that I had had for him for a while—that would be the right way to put it. In two years, we became close. He was the first person in my life to show me what love meant. For the first time, I experienced the warmth of being cared for. I started considering him mine and loved him to the depths. However, some boundaries that I set remained. I never sat on his bike's pillion. Neither did I ever act in ways in which he craved I did, even in intensely romantic moments. That distance was the guardian of our relationship.

Once, when he was unwell, he asked me if I could visit his room. I said I couldn't come alone. 'Come on, I am on my bed, down with fever, not in a position to do you any harm!' he said, with his typical humour. I went, despite my hesitance. I made tea for him and we chatted for a long time. When I was leaving, he thanked me. I left his room that day and my love for him soared much higher. After that, I started visiting his place often.

'Love, I am unable to resist my desire to kiss you. May I? Should there be such restrictions between two individuals like you and me who have decided to be together for life? Please?' he asked me once.

The fact is, even I wanted to kiss him. His love had already won me over—enough to wipe away the physical boundaries I had deliberately set between us. That day, I kissed someone for the first time in my life. Days passed, wearing down the borders between us thinner and thinner. There were none by the time we reached the third year of college. We had sex and lived like a married couple. Our days were sewn together. When the final semester exams commenced, I started experiencing some physical unease. Flouting it, I went on writing the exams well. But I collapsed in the class during my last exam. I could not complete it. The same evening, I visited a doctor.

When I heard what the doctor had to say after investigating me, tears started flowing down my cheeks, strength drained out of every cell in my body. Scared, I ran out of that clinic. I was pregnant; I could not believe it. For that truth to sink in, I repeated what the doctor had just told me. It felt like trying to drown an unsinkable object to an incalculable depth. Uncertain about what to do or where to go, I stood at the bus stop, breaking into sobs. Everything froze in and around that bus shelter. Nothing other than the tears streaming down my face seemed to be moving, not even time. I rang him up sometime later, shaking myself out of that unnerving spell.

'We had used contraceptives; then how did this happen? You don't be scared, dear, I am coming.' Even though he was trying to calm me down, I could sense that he was more terrified than I was. I told him we should let our families know about our relationship immediately and get married soon. Then, for the first time ever, I watched him flare up.

'Are you crazy? I haven't even mentioned you at my home. It's not how it is at your house; convincing my family is an enormous task!'

'We don't have another option, do we? You somehow present our case at home. We will stand our ground.' When I told him this, I saw him grow uptight.

'Marriage is not child's play. Now, please don't start thinking like typical small-town girls. There is a gynaecologist I know; let me ask her,' he said.

I was adamant that I was not going to abort my pregnancy. But, as always, his words had the strength to overpower me.

'To live together, we have to do this now, dear. We are getting married anyway, so don't see this as a big mistake or sin; look at the larger picture and the greater good. This doctor is a close friend of mine. The only problem is that she is a family acquaintance too. So, for now, I can introduce you only as a friend. You please don't feel bad. We will say it was an accident, and you needn't be scared at all.'

Eventually, tired after putting up a lot of resistance, I gave in.

The gynaecologist radiated an air of contempt. The disgust she felt for me and my situation dripped from her words. When I heard her warn him to never come again with such 'sluts' calling for 'help', my heart felt shredded by indignity and grief. I wished to dissolve into a puddle.

I went into a kind of depression. It was a phase where I most anticipated his love and presence. But the landscape of our relationship transformed overnight. Phone calls ceased; he stayed away, saying he needed time to fix everything. Whenever I called his number, it was busy. For the first time, I felt like I was being avoided. The thought scared me. I went to his place and looked for him multiple times, but I could never find him.

Then, one day, I happened to see him with a girl. It was that young lady doctor. When I asked about it, he was elusive. He explained that he had met her to clarify some doubts about my health condition.

Life inched forward, one trying day at a time. That was when I got a phone call.

'Is it something you just started, or have you always been a slut? If that is the case, there are places in Delhi that are better suited for your needs. I am his girlfriend and you better stop bothering him. We have been committed to getting married for a long time. We have pledged to be together for life. I warn you for your own good; you better stop tailing him.'

It was the doctor on the other end of the phone. The world came crashing down around me, making it impossible to say anything in response. I mutely listened to everything she had to say. Right after, I called him up, but his phone was switched off. For countless nights, I kept calling him like a deranged woman. The phone never once rang. Numbly, I stared at the glaring truth right in front of me. Treachery grinned at me; I saw its vampire teeth coming for my throat. I accepted the last thing I would have ever wanted to believe: He was betraying me all the way.

> Joseph, I got betrayed because I loved with my heart and soul. I was called a slut for the same reason. I had seen my child on the sonogram. I killed it; I am a murderer. Can someone get any more wounded than this in the name of love? Unable to bear the pain, I attempted suicide. My friends happened to come by and they rushed me to the hospital. When I gained consciousness in the hospital, I wanted to write to you. But it was only today that they took the bandage off my hand.

I did not have answers for her or a reply that could repaint whatever she underwent and make that picture less ugly. I could only give her my phone number and offer to talk. I spoke to her, assimilating from the books I read and the incidents that pulled me up when my life went downhill. I waited to see her return to life, much more than she did herself.

Over time, we became good friends. She would call occasionally, and every time she did, her calls seemed to veil sadness or fear. That made me realize that the scariest part of being in love isn't the fear of being betrayed or abandoned, but the likelihood that you could end up continuing to love the same person even after they deceive you or do away with you. That possibility looked scary, a loop of perpetual hell from which you may never come out.

I once asked her if she hated him. 'No,' she responded quickly. When I asked whether her love for him was still there somewhere within her, I got a somewhat classic reply.

'If we have ever loved someone intensely, no matter what evil they do to us, your love for them won't be completely gone. You know what I think? This thing we call love gets stored in some part of the brain, where memories never get erased.'

I received a phone call from her some time ago. By the time our conversation ended, I had decided to write this.

'Joseph, he had called. He is marrying her; the date is fixed. The call was not to invite me to the wedding. That girl strongly suspects that we had something going on between us. He loves her a lot. He requested me to tell her there was nothing between me and him.'

'What did you decide?'

'I rang her up. I told her we had nothing going on and that he was only helping a friend in anguish.'

Yes, what she said was true. If we have ever loved someone deeply enough, scarring incidents may diminish our love for them just a little, but it never gets wiped away completely.

Everything said and done, one question remains in my heart, unasked. What would be her answer to the ambassadors of 'sex is not a promise'?

Sitting there, wondering what she would say, I heard the enchanting notes of the beautiful title track of *Mayanadhi* filling the air around me. The timeless, mystical river, with its eternal flow, carries the intertwined stories of a thousand lives marked by love and betrayal.

DADLESS DIGITALISM

'Don't trust everything you see ... Even salt looks like sugar.'

—MARYUM AHSAM

I heard some lies frequently in my years growing up. Looking back, they are downright hilarious. Here are some:

- 'Sanath Jayasuriya's cricket bat has a spring hidden inside it, so he hits sixers at will.'
- 'Indian batsman Navjot Singh Sidhu once killed an umpire by clubbing him in the head.'
- 'Snakes come when you whistle at night.'
- 'The yakshis, Kerala commoner's very own female ghosts, always wear anklets and are clad in white sarees, no matter which day of the week it is.'
- 'If, on the way to school, you happen to see a singular Indian myna, you are surely up for a whacking from the teacher.'
- 'Life will be all good once you finish your studies!'

However, many of those were mostly harmless and thrived owing to the naivety of those times. But lies that we hear today? They would put the yesteryear's lies to shame. Inside the present-day lies lie the real lies—no lying about that!

Social media seems to be a place where lies sell quickly. One may not be wrong to think that the digital world, including YouTube, Facebook or WhatsApp, is what has taught us that lies can be so deep and beautiful.

Here is an example. My mother's sister is a nun who lives in Germany. My maternal family has a WhatsApp group to help all of us keep in touch. It was only recently that my aunt, the nun, got her first smartphone. By default, we added her to the WhatsApp group—'Cousins United'. No, it had nothing much to do with the United States of America or Manchester United; we just needed a cool name. So, in her initial days as a fresh member of 'Cousins United', my aunt maintained stern discipline with her activity in the group. The pictures she forwarded to the group strictly stuck to either some prayer or Jesus himself, and often, they came like tablets, three times a day, before or after food. But one day, a message she forwarded to the group made everyone laugh.

> 'Attention everyone! From now on, please don't buy or consume "Frooti". An AIDS-infected person has somehow managed to mix his blood in the mango drink. Please hurry up and inform your loved ones about this lurking danger!'

In 2007, I received the same 'warning' as a text message, much before we started using WhatsApp extensively. I was a student then, and many of my classmates had received it too. Most of us believed it! I realized that it was a lie only when, much later, I chose to cross-check this piece of information on Google. Ten years later, when I found out that the 'Frooti lie' was still as fresh as a fruity pie, I couldn't help laughing. If it could fool young students ten years ago, I couldn't blame my elderly aunt for falling for it. It was 'the truth' for her until many of us from our family convinced her that it was a baseless piece of information—a lie.

Let us look at something more recent. A good percentage of us fell for this one. A week after the commencement of the Kochi Metro Rail services, one particular piece of 'news' ignited social media. Various headlines screamed:

'Even from an udder full of milk, the mosquito wants only blood! The picture of a drunkard lying asleep in the freshly launched metro rail service goes viral.'

'Keralites won't mend their ways! A passenger on metro rail unconscious from booze.'

'Barely a week into its launch, metro rail is infested by alcoholics. What should be done with these antisocials?'

As soon as this news began surfacing, troll pages took it up. They made memes with the photograph of the person seen with his 'lights off' in the metro rail wagon. Some pages even went to the extent of making derogatory generalizations about the culture of all Malayalis. Two weeks later, another news story raged in all prominent news channels, including Manorama and Mathrubhoomi, like wildfire.

'The truth behind the "drunkard" on the metro.'

The person in the photo was a youngster named Eldo, who was deaf and mute. On that fateful day, his brother was admitted to the Ernakulam General Hospital, critically ill. After visiting his unwell brother, Eldo's young son expressed his innocent wish to travel on the metro on their way home. So, the father-son duo bought tickets to Aluva. While on board, the stress of his brother's condition and overall exhaustion got the better of Eldo, and he dozed off in the comforting air conditioning of the coach. Someone took a photo of the tired man and uploaded it with some harsh captions on Facebook. Some social media pages, revelling in the anonymity of their ownership, made it their fodder for the next day, celebrating 'the drunkard on the metro'. The picture of a young man who was deaf and mute, and who was simply exhausted, went viral. He was unfairly crucified for something he never did.

When the truth emerged, KMRL (Kochi Metro Rail Limited) offered Eldo a Rs 2,000 travel coupon as a gesture of empathy. However, can anything compensate for the humiliation and harassment he and his family endured?

How many such reports reach us every day? If someone asks God about the authenticity of such reports, even God may be tempted to say, 'Only God knows!'

'I habitually urinated under the streetlight every night'—Abraham Lincoln.

If you come across a post like the one above on social media, before commenting something like 'Seems Lincoln's granddad has Malayali roots' or anything else that you find 'funny', please take a moment to consider how reasonable this post is. Would Lincoln have said so or done that? From what we read in more reliable, old-fashioned printed books, the great man *studied* under street lights, right? The point is, for news to grab attention on social media, it needs to have a touch of negativity.

'You will be shell-shocked to know what this man did to a drowning woman!'

When such a piece of news comes up in red font and block letters on your social media page, accompanied by a blurred, ambiguous picture of a woman, it is human tendency to think, 'What would have that scoundrel done to her?'

We click the page and review the complete report to find out what happened. And what do we learn? What did the man do? He saved her!

What else is a man supposed to do when he sees a woman drowning? Buy her a biriyani?

Unfortunately, even positive events garner more attention in the news when presented in malicious wrapping.

Try this exercise; it's simple: Say 'Coca-Cola' without your upper and lower lips touching. You have three attempts. You have failed if you said 'Coca-Cola' on the first try. If you needed two tries, your failure is even worse. If you used all three chances, you have failed beyond any doubt! I know I may sound absurd, but here's the deal: You would have been a winner if you had taken a moment to consider before attempting the task and realized that even if you don't make any effort, your lips won't touch when you say the name Coca-Cola. Where am I taking this long road to? To the good old saying, 'Look before you leap.' In the digital world, look before you leap—be it leaping to conclusions or leaping into action.

Legendary American singer and songwriter Jim Morrison rightly said, 'Whoever controls the media controls the mind.' This statement seems ahead of its time because now, decades later, we know it is an undeniable truth. The media does control us, our minds, our perceptions, our actions and, eventually, our lives.

I was once invited to conduct a session for college students. I was requested to speak about social media's influence on youngsters; so that day, I deviated from my usual presentation style.

'I'll show you some pictures. Please tell me what comes to your mind when you see each one. There's no need to take time to think of something; quickly shout out whatever comes to your mind!' I told the students.

The first picture was a map of the People's Republic of China.

'Population! Cheap Chinese products!' they shouted.

The second picture was that of a solar panel.

After a round of laughter, the replies came with added zeal.

'Saritha! The solar scam! Fraud!'

The final picture was the logo of MRF Tyres.

'Sachin Tendulkar! Virat Kohli!'

Whatever the students shouted, of course, was related to what they saw in the pictures.

But when they saw the map of China, why did the Great Wall of China or Shaolin kung fu not come to their minds? Wasn't China one of the top economies in the world? When it came to the picture of the solar panel, why did the uses of solar power or its significance for the future of the human race not pop up as the first thought? Why was it just the scam and the name of a woman accused of conning many?

What we see and hear most frequently gets registered in our minds. Can the term 'news feeds' be accidental, then? To feed means to provide food or to furnish for consumption. This is what we are consuming—or, to put it another way, this is what our minds are 'eating'.

Buddhism tells us, 'Before you speak, think about three things: Is it necessary? Is it useful? Is it kind?' In this day and age, this three-layered filter seems profound.

We should use the same criteria before we post or propagate something on social media. Firstly, is it helpful to someone? Personally, I categorize anything that doesn't spread hate and makes you laugh as helpful. Each person could have their own standard. Secondly, is it necessary for me to do this now? Third, will it be kind or good or comforting to someone?

On many social media pages, religion and politics are on a rampage. When you look at some posts, you instinctively feel that those hate-mongers should be exiled! Posts from self-proclaimed devotees turn out to be utterly comical at times.

'Type amen and extend your support to Christ while he is staggering with the cross.'

Does God need your help? Even if we assume he does, would typing 'amen' or hitting the 'like' button be helpful?

I can't help but imagine a young Jesus shouting, flicking a whip in his hand, 'Don't waste time typing something or hitting buttons, you dumbheads; go help your mother instead!'

'Unconscionable extravagance at millionaire's marriage. Crores burnt!'

To a news like this, some of us may respond with remarks like, 'Arrogance of affluence!' Or, 'All this when in Africa people die of starvation!'

And so on.

But maybe we need to ask ourselves, 'When I had money and fancied a Hyderabadi biriyani, did I choose to eat two slices of bread instead and buy food for the poor with the cash I saved?'

The easiest thing to do on social media is to criticize others—a controversy involving K.J. Yesudas received widespread attention. The debate centred on a selfie incident. After receiving a national award, as the renowned singer was leaving the event, a young man tried to take a selfie with him without permission. Yesudas immediately stopped, asked the young man for his phone, deleted the picture and returned his phone.

Unsurprisingly, the next day, posts and pictures against the celebrated vocalist began to be celebrated. Videos abusing him and write-ups criticizing him were unleashed. People who were not even born when the man started singing or had any clue what the clamour was about jumped in to make judgements. Despite being only an onlooker, the scenario was embarrassing.

When the pandemonium reached its peak, I couldn't resist doing some googling. I searched for the keywords 'Yesudas Selfie Pictures' and couldn't find a single one. In contrast, I saw plenty of selfies of many other singers. It seemed clear that K.J. Yesudas disliked the concept of selfies. He was even quoted saying, 'Selfies are selfish.' If that's the case, I think it's entirely an individual's prerogative. Whether someone is a celebrity or not is irrelevant here. It's ultimately the choice of a human being like you and me whether we wish to be photographed in a particular way. How can anyone be entitled to question this?

In this incident, the youngster tried to click a selfie with Yesudas without the courtesy of seeking permission first. Would you or I entertain a thing being done to us without our consent, especially if it is something that we are disinclined to? I believe we won't. What the singer did was no different. He may be a celebrity, but he is primarily an individual, a human being with his standpoints and a right to choose. Anyone who forms or circulates such thoughtless responses cuts a sorry figure.

There is nothing complicated here; it is just that we all need to be a little more sensible while handling social media. Kerala is a state that boasts 100 per cent literacy. Shouldn't Keralites lead by example then? Shouldn't there be self-exercised control over speculative posts or inconsiderate responses?

Nowadays, many posts are of unknown origins, as if under some ghostly ownership. What kind of bizarre names have social media pages concocted for themselves? All of them have truckloads of news to dump into our brains. Who is writing these posts? What is their credibility? How sure can we be of all the information we see here? Don't we need to exercise more caution about them, those fatherless pieces of digital information?

Recently, a social media post with Dr P. Gangadharan's picture attached to it came up. It read, 'Things to do to prevent cancer. Foods to eat. Fruits to avoid.' Cancer is still considered the terrible 'Big C', so that post proliferated rapidly on many platforms. Exactly a month later, the doctor published an article in *Mathrubhoomi*, in which he talked about the fake news circulated in his name, and how baseless and misleading such misinformation can be.

With this topic, one can go on and on. But let us wrap it up. Let us remind ourselves of a few things. Media can break lives, turn thieves into saints, promote evil as good and, at some point or the other, make a fool of any of us. Does my social media handle give hope, offer solace, spread love, impart knowledge or create happiness? It is time for each of us to ask this question to the person in the mirror.

In the Malayalam movie *Pathemari*, Mammootty, the great actor, beautifully renders a line that roughly translates to the sentence below.

'If our lives were of help to someone else, that is something we may consider a real achievement.'

Like our lives, may our social media handles also be of some good to someone.

ROMEO MUST LIVE

> 'And once the storm is over, you won't remember how you made it through, how you managed to survive. You won't even be sure whether the storm is really over. But one thing is certain. When you come out of the storm, you won't be the same person who walked in. That's what this storm's all about.'
>
> —HARUKI MURAKAMI, *KAFKA ON THE SHORE*

Clara: I always think of you; you come to mind with each face I see.

Jayakrishnan: The number of faces is just growing with time. So, one day, this one may be forgotten.

Clara: I might forget, right?

Jayakrishnan: Yes.

Clara: But I don't want to.

Here's a memorable conversation from Padmarajan's cult classic, *Thoovanathumbikal*. I remember a note one of my cousins posted on Facebook after reading my first book, *Buried Thoughts*. He wrote, 'I love Joseph's Karla more than Padmarajan's Clara.'

Yes, Karla—that was the name I gave my first love.

'Dude. This Sunday is her wedding, right? That kid had called me up to invite me. Shouldn't we go?' I was engrossed in *I Am Malala*, when Appan nudged me with that question.

'Okay, we shall.' My disinterest was evidenced by the fact that I didn't take my eyes off the book.

'She had specially invited your Amma and me. How about we all go together?'

I shut the book and shot Appan a severe look.

'Appa, are you working on the climax scene for a romantic tragedy? Where are you headed with this? I haven't even decided whether to attend or not. Her invitation may be a matter of courtesy. So, that isn't reason enough for all of us to dive in together!'

'Why? You're sad or what?' Appan enquired. The question was asked with a playful yet genuine tone, and Appan sported a mischievous grin as he took that dig at me.

'Come on, Appa! Don't annoy me. It's been six long years since it was over. Now, what is left to be sad about? You know everything! Why spoil my mood then?'

'Dude, you know what I think? I think you better be sad! If not, what kind of a pathetic lover were you? If you are the guy you are today, she too has played a role in shaping it. It was her love that inspired you to write for the first time. I was very fond of her. Your Amma and I will definitely be attending her wedding. If you come along, I can assure you that it will be one of the most unique experiences of your life.'

I didn't say anything in response. Appan stood up and placed his palm on my shoulder.

'Moreover, I think she will be expecting you,' he said quietly and made his way into the kitchen.

Was I feeling sad?

Not very much, to be honest. Her love was like a sudden downpour; it drenched me, and washed a lot of dirt and stains off me. Looking back, I see her like beautiful rain—one that had ceased long ago, but the memories she left continue to drizzle over me, trickling from some solitary branch, twig or leaf of my soul. Our love felt like the lingering scent of monsoon, enduring long after the last drop had dried up.

'Er ... We shall go together,' I said, with not much conviction in my voice.

'Are you not telling him the other bit?' Amma asked Appan. I hadn't noticed her standing there until then.

'Listen. Amma has a wish ...' Appan shifted his glance between Amma and me.

'What wish?'

'She wants to buy a gift for the bride. I have some long-overdue shopping as well; I need to get myself a pair of shirts and some trousers. So why not club this together? Would the writer be kind enough to take some time off tomorrow?' Appan asked.

Appan uses the tactic of addressing me as 'the writer' when he proposes something that I am likely to say no to. The term 'writer' reminds me in advance that if I decline whatever it is, I am giving them the opportunity to accuse me of 'having changed' after finding success as a writer.

'At the marriage majority may mostly mock me as mawkish, mushy, maudlin and movie-like, mind you! Anyway, if that's how you both want it, I shall come along, and we shall all go,' I said.

They simply thanked me and left as if they hadn't heard a word from the first sentence. I shouldn't have wasted time alliterating with M.

On Saturday morning, Appan and I started from home. When we reached the Angamaly traffic signal, Appan suggested that we go shopping at the biggest mall in the area. We had a long shopping list, so I agreed, knowing it would help us get back home quicker.

When we entered the complex, I headed for the fourth floor, as always. But then I noticed Appan going straight to a jewellery store on the first floor. I ran down the stairs towards him.

'Appa, the shirts and trousers you need are on the fourth floor, in the men's stores there.'

Seeing his smile, it became clear that his entrance into the jewellery store was no mistake.

'Uh oh, what are you up to?' I asked.

'Me and Amma have decided to buy her a golden ring,' he declared.

I paused for a moment to fully comprehend what I had just heard. This was coming from someone who always pounced on me whenever I bought even the smallest of gifts for a friend. Unprecedented magnanimity!

'Your Amma and I feel we must do this. You needn't bother. Go and do your shopping. I prefer selecting the ring myself.'

Unsure of what to say, I just nodded.

In the Malayalam movie *Charlie*, there's a scene in which the elderly character, played by actor Nedumudi Venu, meets his long-lost love fortuitously and tells Charlie, 'I need to be alone for some time.' Charlie responds to the request with an unusual smile. He was experiencing a new kind of happiness, different from anything he had felt so far in life. While walking to the fourth floor, leaving Appan in the jewellery store, I experienced a joy similar to what I imagine Charlie felt in the movie.

Until a moment ago, I was least emotional. I knew it was her wedding tomorrow but wasn't very sad. I had swum across that pain through the years, with toil and time blunting its edges. I had succeeded in forgetting it, at least the prickly part of it. So, what I was feeling was not sadness. Before leaving the jewellery store, I saw my elderly father, filled with pure, childlike enthusiasm, ask the salesperson, 'Please show me the newest models of gold rings.'

The image evoked fresh emotion within me. She loved hearing me talk about Appan. Was it because her dad was terror in human form or had she just grown used to me always speaking about my Appan? I don't know. But one thing I am sure of is that she adored Appan. She would call up on every birthday of his. On some, she had even sent him gifts.

The next day, Appan, Amma and I attended her wedding. Her mother addressed me as 'son' and hugged me. Enacting the role of some surrealistically sweet father, my otherwise sarcastic Appan beckoned me up the stage.

Of all the times I had seen her, it was on the day of her wedding that I found her the most beautiful.

'Jo, you have grown handsome, haven't you?' she remarked with her typical innocent giggle. 'Oh, I think I understand now. You've become a successful writer, making arriving here on time for the marriage ceremony impossible. It's great that you've managed to make it at least by lunch!' She kept teasing me, all in good spirits.

Appan was right about it being a unique experience. I was feeling something entirely new. I might not be able to describe it to you accurately, but there is one thing I can say for sure: It wasn't grief.

Appan and Amma followed me to the stage. She hugged Appan. Amma took the ring from her handbag and handed it to her mother.

'This is a small gift from Joseph,' I heard Amma tell her.

Warmth and affection were palpable on her mother's face.

She introduced me to her daughter's husband, 'They were classmates. He is like a son to me.'

We shook hands. All of us took a photograph together.

'Dear God, I pray that she is blessed with nothing but happiness in life,' I uttered in a moment of prayer. Wishing the newlyweds a happy married life, we exited the venue.

While in the car, on our way back home, nobody spoke for a long time.

'How is it?' Appan asked, breaching a long hush.

'What?'

'As in, how does it feel?'

The car was stuck at a traffic signal and I was still filled with an overwhelming sense of bliss throughout our journey back.

'This climax was fantabulous, Appa. You scripted it impeccably. If this was a movie scene, I bet this would have received a standing ovation!'

Appan laughed.

'Son, it is only now that the lover boy you played in this story has come out as a true hero!'

In the rearview mirror, I could see Amma smiling ear to ear.

The traffic signal changed from red to green. I moved forward.

FRIENDSHIP, LOVE, LIFE

'In three words, I can sum up everything I've learned about life:
It goes on.'

—ROBERT FROST

It was prayer time at Parish Church, led by a well-known man in our locality. The service progressed with songs, Bible verses and hymns.

'Now comes the time for confession. Keep your left palm on your heart and raise your right hand. Recall the sins you have committed and confess. If you have hurt your parents, made fun of your teachers, fallen in love with someone from a different religion—seek God's pardon. Being in love is also a sin because the one who is in love has already allied with the devil.' The man then proceeded to cite a Bible verse and stated that love was a sin. I put my hands down, crossed myself, stood up and exited the church. But before I left, I prayed, 'Dear God, they don't know what they are doing. Please pardon them.'

Back in 2015, I had to travel to Mumbai for a work assignment. Over there, I had to meet a Sandeep Kumar Singh, who was based in our company's Mumbai branch, and accompany him as we travelled around the city to do 'potential customer mapping'. By then, I had been dissatisfied with my job for about three years. I struggled to make a firm decision because I knew I needed the money to survive, but, at the same time, I felt a strong urge to pursue what I truly loved. It often felt like I was torn between these two conflicting parts of myself, leaving me feeling constantly reflective and trapped in melancholy.

When my boss, Jinoj, asked me to go to Mumbai, I felt secretly happy, unlike in the past. The reason was that I had recently finished reading *Shantaram* by Gregory David Roberts. It tells the story of a man who escapes from an Australian prison, comes to India with a fake passport and soon becomes involved in the notorious Mumbai underworld. He comes to be known as the 'gentleman thief'. The novel narrates how this man, with a deep-seated goodness in his heart that never completely dries up, becomes beloved by the people living on Mumbai's streets. I've heard that in Mumbai, there is even a tour package called 'Shantaram Tourism'. It takes you to where the man lived, the roads he travelled and the spots he chose for his meetings.

The Gateway of India has always drawn tourists, over the years. But after the 26/11 terror attacks, this city became a destination for dark tourism, which involves travelling to places associated with death and suffering. When I met Sandeep Kumar Singh, I told him I wanted to visit Leopold Café.

'Joseph, Leopold Café is a place that most of my friends who visit Mumbai want to see. In the terror attack, ten people, including one foreign national, a woman, were killed at Leopold Café. The marks made by the bullets that the terrorists shot can still be seen on the walls. It was an incident that rattled this city! I shall for sure take you there.'

By then, Sandeep seemed to have taken on the responsibility of being my tourist guide.

'Thanks, Sandeep! The reason I want to visit Leopold Café has nothing to do with the terror attack. I want to go there because of a book called *Shantaram* that had a great impact on me. It's about an Australian prisoner who escapes jail and comes to Mumbai with a fake passport. He learns Hindi and Marathi, and becomes involved with the city's underworld. He used to conduct all his business at Leopold Café and I heard that there was even a chair reserved just for him. As far as I know, it might still be there!'

Sandeep had never heard about *Shantaram*. The excitement of having shaken hands with a new tale about his beloved city was evident in him; his face lit up.

'After hearing this, I also feel like reading *Shantaram*. The last customer we have lined up for today is at Colaba. Leopold Café is also at Colaba, and near it is a market where they sell books at cheaper rates. We will go there, as well.'

Around 5 p.m., we boarded our taxi to Colaba. We had to walk a short distance to the café from where the taxi had dropped us off. While walking, my mind was actively rebuilding the images of the café that the book had described. Within a few moments, I saw that board: 'Leopold Café and Bar, since 1871'. Inadvertently, my stride grew faster.

As soon as I entered, I was greeted by stacks of *Shantaram*, neatly arranged.

'Sandeep, this is the book I was talking about! Are you buying a copy for yourself?'

Sandeep took one copy out, placed it flat on his palm, and moved it up and down twice.

'This book is quite large. I was expecting a smaller one,' he admitted, gesturing with his thumb and forefinger the thickness of the book he had in mind.

'Anyway, I will buy myself a copy from the book market; they offer better prices there,' he said.

Happy after a productive day at work and a visit to the fabled café, we decided to each have a can of beer. As we drank, I enthusiastically shared more about the book, this time with unbridled eloquence, narrating some exciting sequences from the book. When I revealed that they were based on the author's real-life experiences, Sandeep's jaw dropped.

While making our way out of the café, I took one copy of *Shantaram* and casually riffled through the pages. As if serendipitously, the line I saw on the page I randomly opened was one I had underlined in my own copy while reading it—my favourite line from the novel.

'The choice you make, between hating and forgiving, can become the story of your life.'

When we stepped out, I noticed that the setting felt unusually red. Red all around: Red balloons, decorations with red glitter, red ribbons, red roses, red dresses … Everything looked red, redder and reddest. That was when it dawned on me that it was 14 February, Valentine's Day.

'Joseph, how about we go to Marine Drive? On this day, you could see all the lovebirds of Mumbai there. And, if we are fortunate, some hot scenes too!' Sandeep winked at me.

When I looked around, everything seemed to confirm Sandeep's description. He told me that Marine Drive was known as the 'queen's necklace' because the lights along the C-curve of the beach twinkled at night, resembling a necklace. Countless couples sat facing the sea, all of them appearing very happy. Some leaned against each other, some held hands and some kissed. Sandeep was on a call. He left me alone to enjoy the sunset and take in all the romance in the air.

Thus, I sat there, looking at the crows and the sunset beneath them. The crows seemed to care nothing about the sunset, though. That was when a small boy walked up to me with a rose in his hand.

'Valentine's Day rose, sir! Dus rupaiya, sir!'

He persuaded me to purchase it by gently brushing my face with a red rose.

'Dear boy, I have no one to give this to! Can't you see that I am sitting alone?' I wished to tell him this in Hindi, but I could barely speak the language.

With my palms open and facing him, and moving my arms like the windscreen wipers of a car, I managed to convey to him that I didn't need a rose. The boy took the rose back and added it to his bunch. As he moved to the next customer, I couldn't help but notice the look on his face. It seemed like confusion regarding my gestures and maybe even pity because I was single on Valentine's Day. Then he vanished into the crowd, as if in a magic trick, and I lost sight of him. That image of the little boy and the rose he offered me remains fresh in my mind, just like the scent of that flower.

On a majestic pillar of light, the sun slowly rappelled down. A single glance at that glorious retreat was enough to make anyone homesick. In the company of a cool, caressing sea breeze, I closed my eyes to meditate on my share of long-lost love.

I fell in love with them during different periods of my life, and I truly believe my love for both was unalloyed. However, I'm left wondering why I didn't end up with either. These two women entered my life at different stages of my youth, leaving me with cherished memories that still make me smile at the mere whiff of those times. Yet, neither of them is with me on this day of love.

'The answer is simple: I did not love them enough. I just thought I did. And perhaps neither of them really loved me, either. We probably enormously liked each other, which we mistook for love.'

Maybe the real reasons are still unclear beneath the fog of my conclusions. Whenever I discussed this with any of my friends or family, the responses I received were the clichéd, traditional ones handed down from generation to generation. There was always a set of responses used only when talking about love failures and most of them had their appeal, but my favourite one had to be: 'Your soul mate, the love of your life, is waiting for you somewhere. Nothing but her prayers make you keep failing with the wrong ones!'

When I felt the void of lost love, life always filled it with amazing friendships. I've been fortunate to have rich friendships, not only with my friends but also with my family.

'Friendship is a bridge that helps a man to walk across his loneliness.' This is one of the best lines I have ever read about friendship. Without the richness of friendships I have enjoyed, I would have experienced the agonizing poverty that arises from a scarcity of good friends.

The words of a Bangladeshi neurosurgeon came to mind at that moment: 'Just counting your blessings is enough to take you to eternal bliss.' As the tantalizing twilight stood watching, I started counting my blessings. I thought about my parents, who always showered me with love and affection in everything they gave me. Being the youngest of the lot, I always had my two older brothers standing on either side, taking care of me. I also had great friends who were always there to accommodate my whims and listen to me. And then there were the two lovely women who walked out of my life without wishing me any harm. Lastly, the great people who came into my life from the moment I picked up my pen. The list continued, like a red carpet rolling out in my mind, welcoming a wholehearted smile to spread across my face.

But I couldn't ignore the frightening void lurking behind all these blessings. What was I seeking? Love? What exactly is love?

Of all the couples I see swarming this beach, how many are really in love? If the desire is anything less than to be together 'till death do us part', I believe we are not really in love. The rest seem to be offshoots of elemental human curiosity or needs of one kind or the other.

My friend Hrishikesh once told me something about travel.

'Joseph, it doesn't mean much to say that you have visited a lot of lands. What matters is whether or not you carried back the essence of their souls with you. There is a huge difference between being acquainted with a person and truly knowing them. The first can be as easy as a hello exchanged. But the second is a long journey. You may have to walk unending miles.'

Many a time, love affairs seem to be a misinterpretation of familiarity. There is nothing profound to them, sort of 'touch and go'.

Real love will continue to get slaughtered as long as there are men who can't express love with their clothes on and women who see love as just a way to pass time. Many of them put up well-tailored performances with beautiful masks on. Sometimes, I feel a weighty sense of loss, as if I haven't truly experienced love in its purest form. My encounters with love were like those of a man who thinks he knows the ocean just by watching the tides and counting the waves from the shore. For me, love is that ocean. The mysterious calm in its middle, the unfathomable depths and the unending awe it inspires—none of these have I known. It's as if someone asks if you've seen the ocean and you reply, 'Sort of.' Have I ever been in love? No. I have experienced only the shore, the waves and the tides. I've never loved anyone as deeply as the ocean nor have I been loved in that way.

Despite having numerous reasons to feel happy, why does our mind consistently gravitate towards the love yet to be discovered? Why does it continue to dwell in this sadness? There were moments when I even prayed, 'Dear God, grant me the opportunity to experience genuine love just once; allow me to comprehend the profoundness of this miracle.'

When someone claims that humans are the greatest of God's creations, I can't help but laugh. How insignificant are we? Even when we have everything we could ever want, our eyes only see the flaws. We see sadness and loneliness, and we are content with nothing. I believe that only the deepest love can salvage a human being. We need to be deeply in love with something in our short lives! Whether it's a partner, books, a career, music or something else! I think it's impossible to find lasting happiness without being deeply in love.

The suicide note of the great poet Edappally Raghavan Pillai read:

> To have something to work on, have someone to love, have something to wish for, in these three things lie the root of every joy in this world. All I have is disappointment and my only egress: death. I am embracing it with happiness. No one is at a loss in this blissful departure, but I gain. No one is responsible for this, even by a thought, a word, or a deed. May the suspicion of society or the unforgiving sword of the law not fall on innocence! I wish to sing, but my flute is broken. Adieu.

A man ended his life because he had nothing to work towards, no one to love and nothing to wish for. Do his words scare you? Love is the only way out of this fear. Love for life!

There is a WhatsApp forward I think about a lot:

> The job you complain about is somebody's dream,
> Your cranky child is the dream of someone who has none,
> The homeless dreams of having a small one like yours someday,
> A man drowning in debts can't even dream of your little savings,
> Your health is the dream of the dying,
> And your smile is the farthest dream of someone sad!

Your life takes a turn at the point you start finding reasons to love it. That night, while walking through the streets of Mumbai with my friend Sandeep Kumar Singh, there was one thing my mind was yearning to do: Write.

'Joseph, this is the book market. You can buy books at really cheap rates. But you should bargain with no hesitation at all! If you can get

Shantaram for a hundred rupees, buy a copy for me. I need to go and make another phone call. Valentine's Day duties, brother!' Sandeep walked away with a naughty smile.

I found myself standing in the middle of hundreds of thousands of books, each a magical creation by a soul that had fallen in love with letters! As I stood there, the desire to write started to well up within me. I sat on a bench beside a heap of books and took out my laptop. Feeling the presence of countless writers, I rediscovered my fondness for writing, which I had lost somewhere along the way. I prayed to God to turn that fondness into love and to make my love for writing an unquenchable fire. And then, as if after an eternity, I scribbled three words.

Friendship. Love. Life.

ABOUT THE AUTHOR AND TRANSLATOR

Joseph Annamkutty Jose is a bestselling Indian author, motivational speaker and media personality from Kerala. Rising to fame as an RJ with Radio Mirchi, he became widely known for his inspirational storytelling, social commentary and thought-provoking speeches.

His books, with over 300,000 copies sold in Malayalam, have deeply resonated with readers, while his 3 million+ social media followers turn to him for motivation and empowerment. Honoured as one of India's 75 Cultural Brand Ambassadors, he was also invited by the US Department of State for the International Visitor Leadership Program (IVLP) for his contributions to media.

A highly sought-after speaker, Joseph's engaging, humorous and deeply impactful talks on self-growth, resilience and mental health continue to inspire audiences worldwide.

Hrishikesh Mundani is a screenwriter, lyricist and actor whose work spans the web, television and film network. During his stint away from visual media as Radio Mirchi's creative writer, he ventured into the kaleidoscopic world of radio copies, sparklers, jingles and voice-overs. Hrishikesh is now part of the quality control team at Warner Bros. Discovery, focusing on content customization.

HarperCollins *Publishers* India

At HarperCollins India, we believe in telling the best stories and finding the widest readership for our books in every format possible. We started publishing in 1992; a great deal has changed since then, but what has remained constant is the passion with which our authors write their books, the love with which readers receive them, and the sheer joy and excitement that we as publishers feel in being a part of the publishing process.

Over the years, we've had the pleasure of publishing some of the finest writing from the subcontinent and around the world, including several award-winning titles and some of the biggest bestsellers in India's publishing history. But nothing has meant more to us than the fact that millions of people have read the books we published, and that somewhere, a book of ours might have made a difference.

As we look to the future, we go back to that one word—a word which has been a driving force for us all these years.

Read.